TESTIMONIALS

What Parents, Educators, Kids, and Other Authors Are Saying About Dana Arias and

DEAR PARENTS,
From Your Child's Loving Teacher:

"I think it is great that you are teaching students how to be assertive and understand that their actions have consequences. I think it is important for children to realize we are entitled to make our own decisions and that there are options. This way, kids, hopefully, will think twice about something and not fall into 'peer pressure' now or later on in life."

Sandra Herrera
Teacher and Mother

"You honor children and parents throughout each letter. You give concrete examples of how to communicate, how to develop study habits, how to listen, and really, how to love. All parents love their kids, but they don't have the experience that you have with teaching, learning, and loving altogether. I hear your voice and feel your spirit throughout each letter. Onward!"

Susan Kilbane
Principal, New Field School

"Even though I do not have children, your book helped me visualize what kind of parent I want to be and how I can achieve it. I truly believe I will use the strategies you described with my own children. Time is the greatest gift, and I really appreciate you taking the time to write your book. Awesome, Awesome Work, Dana!"

Ryan Hammond
Physical Education Teacher

"This book is wonderful! What an invaluable resource for parents. I love the letter format, which makes it easy for busy parents to gain insightful strategies at their own pace. I appreciate the book's encouraging tone that supports parents and promotes a strong home-school connection, which we know is so critical for our students' learning and development. Excellent work!"

Rebecca Sinclair
Special Education Teacher (Autism)

"In her well-uttered letters, Miss Arias warmly captures a way to approach parents and children, with each creating a simple understanding on pedagogical methods, how to make a good use out of them, and how to apply them easily to increase children's capacity. Each important tip is well described here and graphically explained, making this book a great ally and an effortless-to-follow guide for parents."

Barbara Cardenas
Mother of Four

"I am going to tell you what I learned from you. Well, the first thing I learned from you is a very nice thing. What you told me was to believe in myself, and if I make a mistake, it is okay because I learn from my mistakes."

C.G.
Third Grade Student

"You are the best teacher because you like us and love us."

A.P.

Third Grade Student

"I learned about how to respect other people."

A.H.

ESL, Third Grade Student

"Your conversational approach to exploring children's learning in relation to parenting skills can be utilized by a wide array of parents. Educators like you prove that the importance of recognizing parents as teachers is vital to the learning cycle."

Miranda Jimenez

Community School Coordinator, SGA Youth and Family Services

"Thanks for all the effort you put into not just teaching the kids, but communicating with parents to help the children grow in their literacy, make good choices, be responsible, and become more ethical young adults. I believe you act like a partner by reaching out to parents as well as children."

Jillana Enteen

Co-Director, NU Digital Humanities Lab Northwestern University

"We, the parents and community volunteers, would like to express what a joy and a learning experience it is to be around and assist Ms. Arias. She is a great resource to us all. Encouraging us to learn, giving us books, translating for us, and she always has kind words."

Virgen Torres Martillo, Ana Hernandez, Maria Oliveros, Sandra Ruiz, Areli Gutierez, Elizabeth Ruiz

Parents and Community Volunteers

"After reading *Dear Parents*, I feel that I have a clearer idea of the challenges my students and their families face every day, and confidence that, with the guidance of Dana Arias, children and adults alike will cultivate compassion and fortitude in their work and play."

Shana Harvey
Teaching Artist with the Ravinia Festival

"Ms. Arias' book is so approachable. It takes the mystery out of why teachers ask parents to do the things they do, and it explains how simple things can make a big difference in your daily life and your child's future. This book isn't about making kids better learners; it's about making families stronger and parents and teachers better partners."

Cathleen Andes
Teacher and Parent

"Dana Arias embodies positive energy. As she continues on her path to self-fulfillment, she enriches those around her. It is an honor to call Dana a life friend and a bonus to have her as a colleague."

Laura Hurtt
Teacher and Mother

"Too often in education, stakeholders blame each other for inadequate student achievement. This book not only helps bridge the gap between parents and teachers, but it gives specific ideas for creating a culture of open, constructive communication with children."

Dan Dusel
Teacher

"*Dear Parents* is a beautifully written book of letters from a teacher to her students' parents that not only shows Dana Arias' care and compassion for parents and students both, but it will open up communication between everyone involved in a child's learning processes and make them better understand how that learning takes place throughout their school years. Every child should be so lucky as to have a teacher like Dana Arias!"

Tyler R. Tichelaar, Ph.D.
Award-Winning Author of *The Best Place*

"This book is filled with great wisdom and practical help on a subject that affects teachers everywhere. It's a 'must read' for every parent with school age kids."

Susan Friedmann, CSP
International Best-Selling author of
Riches in Niches: How to Make it BIG in a small Market

Handbook for Effective Teamwork

DEAR PARENTS

From Your Child's Loving Teacher

Dana Arias

Dear Parents
From Your Child's Loving Teacher

Copyright©2013 by Dana M. Arias

All Rights Reserved. No part of this book may be used or reproduced in any manner whatsoever without the express written permission of the author.

Address all inquiries to:
Dana M. Arias
Dana@DanaArias.com
www.DanaArias.com
www.DearParentsBook.com

ISBN: 978-1-938686-64-1
Library of Congress Control Number: 2013943925
Copyright Number (TXu 1-848-401)

Editor: Tyler Tichelaar
Cover Design: Bonnie Richter
Interior Book Design: Fusion Creative Works

Every attempt has been made to source properly all quotes.

Printed in the United States of America

First Edition
2 4 6 8 10

For additional copies visit: www.DearParentsBook.com

Transformation always begins from within. Thank you, parents, for always being a reminder to me of what the power of love can transform. As you transform yourself, you will transform your children.

There is always a silver lining of hope for all that we desire.

– Dana Arias

DEDICATION

When I think of all the people who have touched my life, I realize I am truly blessed. My life has been enriched by all of the interactions I have ever experienced. Some have been kind and loving, fun and exhilarating, others thorny and painful. Yet, the ones that have helped me grow and develop into the person I am have been a mixture of them all. And it is here, where I find myself touching a silver lining, that I never stopped believing. This silver lining would not be possible if it were not for all of you who have helped me in all of my endeavors, so to each one of you, I dedicate this book with love and gratitude.

Mom and Dad, you taught me the power of perseverance. Through every adversity, you showed me that love conquers all. There is nothing that can't be conquered with love. Even in the darkest hours, the love you had for each other shone as a beacon of hope for our family and held us together. Therefore, this book is dedicated to both of you, and Jorge, Johnny, and Lydia. I love you all.

Oscar, without you this book could have not been written. Your quiet and not-so-quiet support allowed me to move forward. Every day, you allowed me to sit at the computer for hours, and you sat and listened to my letters and gave your opinions. You showed me a side of parenthood that was very foreign to me. You taught me that parents can transform themselves because they love. Thank you for being my strongest supporter, best friend, and partner. I love you.

Danita and Michael, you chose to follow my guidance, sometimes with ease and love, and sometimes not. The results have brought us together as a family. More importantly, you have allowed me to experience motherhood at its fullest. Without your help, I would not have been able to gain the insights I have shared with my readers. Thank you for being who you are. I love you both.

Leti, you were the first teacher to take me by the hand and guide me. Your example, mentorship, and friendship have shaped me into the teacher I am. Yet, you were the first of many. My life has been blessed with so many wonderful teachers. Each one has contributed to this book in his or her own unique way. Cathleen, you held my hand through the whole process. Laura, you proofread and corrected. Eduardo, you helped me keep the faith when starting my writing process. Ryan and Becky, you believed and you let me know you did. For your friendship and faith, I thank you and all the wonderful teachers who touch the lives of students everywhere. We are the changing force that sometimes is not recognized for what it is. Let us hold our heads up high and be proud of what we are, **teachers**.

Finally, I owe a huge debt of gratitude to every student I have ever had, in and out of the classroom. Without knowing it, you have been my greatest teachers. Thank you.

And I owe a debt to the parents of those students. Without your help, I never would have known the important needs your children had as well as your devotion to helping your children succeed in the classroom. And it goes without saying that without you, I never would have written this book.

It is with joy that I can claim a rich and loving life—one filled with many experiences that have led me to touch a silver lining. May each and every one of you, my readers, find the silver lining in your life.

To you all, I dedicate this book with love and gratitude,

Lovingly,

Dana M. Arias

ACKNOWLEDGMENTS

Gratitude is a gift. Its true meaning lies in the many blessings that life bestows upon us. Therefore, I only find it fitting to share my deepest gratitude with all of you who have supported my efforts as I wrote this book. Without your help and encouragement, this book would not be as rich as it is. Each one of you helped me stay on track and not lose my way. Thank you for your love and support.

Parents, this book came to be because of your constant questions. Thank you for asking. You inspired and moved me to write. Your questions are the heart and soul of this book.

Leti, you taught me how to be a teacher. Many of the lessons in this book are here because of your guidance.

Cathleen, your continuous support definitely makes you the aunt of this book. I know you understand.

Laura and Eduardo, you believed in my book when I was getting started.

Ryan and Becky, your willingness to read it in its initial stages and your constant positive encouragement kept me writing.

Ms. Kilbane and all of my New Field family, this book reflects the culture of respect, collaboration, and responsibility that we have achieved at our school. Thank you for being who you are and contributing so much to our school and students. Most of all, thank you for being the constant support that you are to me.

Señora Araceli, Señora Isabel, and Señora Antonia, thank you for your unconditional support. Your love and kindness shines through in every page of this book.

Señora Escalante, you reunited me with Helena and have always been a loving aunt to me.

Helena, you listened to my dream and found me a coach.

Patrick Snow, you have made this process such a simple one. Your help and guidance have been invaluable. Without you, this book would not be what it is.

Tyler Tichelaar, you have taken my book and dressed it up, making the words flow and read beautifully.

Bonnie Richter, you listened carefully to my idea and created a book cover I love.

Shiloh Schroeder, you took all of the components of a book and made them a book. Wow!

Susan Friedmann, I've heard it is hard to find a publishing company. This has not been my experience. You have been kind and generous.

Greg Anderson, you made the printing experience a simple one.

Jorge, you taught me to believe in my writing abilities.

Patricia, Alyssa, and Georgia, you sat through eternal readings of my letters and told me what you honestly thought.

Michael, your patience with my computer problems saved the day every time.

Danita, you learned how to listen, truly listen, and supported me.

Oscar, you held me through thick and thin. Your love and support have been the thread that is woven through this entire book.

To each and every one of you, thank you. Your love and support is the richest gift I could have asked for as I traveled the world of authorship.

CONTENTS

Foreword by Patrick Snow — 19
Introduction: Creating a New Beginning for Parents and Teachers — 25
Letter 1: Learning Skills and Dinner—How They Connect — 31
Letter 2: Learning How to Listen — 33
Letter 3: Encouraging as We Learn to Listen — 37
Letter 4: Listening Creates Strong Family Bonds — 39
Letter 5: Listening to Our Own Needs Actually Benefits the Family — 43
Letter 6: Taking Care of You Is Not Selfish! It Is Necessary — 47
Letter 7: Putting Parents' True Needs First Can Teach Gratitude — 49
Letter 8: Teaching Our Children Values Through Small Moments — 53
Letter 9: Learning to Self-Regulate and Communicate — 57
Letter 10: Connecting Our Ideas and Oral Language to Writing Is the Key to Success — 61
Letter 11: Writing Helps Clear Our Thoughts — 65
Letter 12: Writing Helps Us Discover Our Voice — 69
Letter 13: Thinking Levels: How Do We Develop Them? — 75
Letter 14: Building New Ideas: As We Learn and Think — 79
Letter 15: Thinking Levels in the Classroom — 85
Letter 16: How the Thinking Process Develops as Children Grow — 91

Letter 17: Measuring Thinking Levels with Tests — 99
Letter 18: Developing Your Child's Thinking Skills — 103
Letter 19: Helping Your Child Explore His or Her Own Ideas — 107
Letter 20: Engaging in Fun Activities That Help Learning — 111
Letter 21: Learning Activities That Foster Thinking — 115
Letter 22: Connecting Ideas and Writing — 121
Letter 23: Setting Boundaries Is Important — 125
Letter 24: Developing Language Skills — 129
Letter 25: Developing Stories and Creativity — 133
Letter 26: Developing Your Child's Brain — 137
Letter 27: Putting Our Ideas Into Writing — 141
Letter 28: Setting Up Expectations and the Will to Persevere — 147
Letter 29: Teaching Our Children Perseverance — 153
Letter 30: Developing Responsibility and Discipline: Whose Job Is It? — 161
Letter 31: Educating vs. Teaching—The Value of Following Through — 165
Letter 32: Teaching Perseverance Through Homework — 169
Letter 33: Finding Strength to Set Boundaries — 175
Letter 34: Taking Control by Setting Good and Functional Boundaries — 181
Letter 35: Teaching Through Consequences and Confrontation — 187
A Final Note — 195
About the Author — 201
Coaching — 205
Book Dana Arias to Speak at Your Next Event — 207

FOREWORD

Growing up and attending school in the '70s and '80s, I was often labeled as someone who struggled with reading comprehension and speaking issues. I remember being placed in the slow reading group, and I never really enjoyed reading aloud in class because I did not sound as fluent as some of the other students who were in the more advanced reading groups. I often wondered why I struggled as a reader as a young child, and why others did not.

What I discovered was that when a teacher took a personal interest in my success and allowed me to pursue or read on the subject matters that I enjoyed, I blossomed as a student, and ultimately many years later, I became a best selling author and professional speaker because of the teachers and coaches who took an interest in me, challenged me beyond my self-imposed limits, and loved me as if I were their own child.

As a result, I believe that children will experience success in the classroom when they are loved, challenged, and nourished. Most importantly, children succeed in school when adults believe in them. In fact, psychologist, author, and motivational speaker Dr. Robert Brooks has been quoted as saying:

> *"One of the most important factors that contributes to the resilience in children is the presence of at least one person in their lives who believes in them."*

In this powerful book written by Dana Arias, you will learn how parents and teachers can work together in the spirit of harmony for the benefit of their students and children alike. A very successful and bilingual teacher and librarian, Dana has spent years and years nurturing, challenging, and believing in her students, all the while communicating to their parents what they can do as well to allow their children to flourish as students and grow academically. In Dana's school district in Chicago, students come from sixty countries and speak forty different languages so this book is proven to work regardless of the socioeconomic background of you and your family, your language, and your location. Most importantly, Dana *believes* in the potential of your child, and this book will help you strengthen your level of belief in your child!

In *Dear Parents*, Dana offers you a series of letters, which are basically an ongoing conversation, that can help you as the parent better prepare your student to succeed academically. These letters provide you, the parent, with the tools you need to work together with your children's teachers to create twenty-first century learners. When you and your child follow the wisdom and advice offered in this book, your children will become confident students achieving grades higher than ever before. And more important than the grades will be their desired thirst for ongoing and continuous learning, for exploring, for understanding that they can achieve any dream, any goal that their hearts have in store for them.

These strategies, tools, and techniques are proven to work with your child. After all, Dana is not just a librarian and teacher herself; she is also the parent of two teenagers, so she can completely understand and empathize with you and your challenges that you face daily in raising a family, working a job, and constantly juggling all the things that pull you in opposite directions.

Throughout this book, you will get nuggets of wisdom from Dana that you can apply to your sons and daughters so they can grow into the students they are potentially capable of becoming. These letters will set your mind at ease, and when their advice is followed, amazing results can be experienced by the child, while both parents and teachers can be assured that their efforts are being acknowledged and recognized.

So sit back, read this book, and then read it again! Share this book with all of the other parents in your school district, your PTO organization, and your neighborhood. Apply the wisdom of this teaching to your children and watch amazing things happen as the result. Get ready for an exciting journey. Your life as a parent has just gotten easier, and your children are about to take their academic experiences and soar to new heights.

Patrick Snow

Patrick Snow
International Best-Selling Author of *Creating Your Own Destiny* and *The Affluent Entrepreneur*
www.PatrickSnow.com

INTRODUCTION

Creating a New Beginning for Parents and Teachers

Today, many people complain about kids behaving obnoxiously. They are under the impression that these kids seem to think they are entitled and, therefore, exhibit selfish behaviors. Many even say that the kids are a reflection of their parents. When one looks closer, these kids do seem to be a reflection of their parents' upbringing. Some parents might say, "I do not teach my child to behave that way." The problem is that most likely those parents did and are not aware of it. Yes, that bratty kid is their creation! There is no denying it, like it or not, the child is behaving and acting as taught by his or her parents.

Now, don't pretend that you don't know what I am talking about; you know that what I am saying is true. We all hope that no one sees our child as that bratty kid. But maybe people do because, after all, we know what problems we have at home and at school. What if your child is thought of as that kid?

So now you are starting to worry about this little problem of yours. What are you to do? It is affecting your home life, and your child's teacher keeps telling you she is having problems with the little one. You want to tell the teacher you're drowning, but you can't. Why is it that she keeps complaining? Why did she fail him? That grade was not fair! Who does she think she is? Why does she send so much homework? Isn't she doing her job? If she were, then your sweet little one would behave, right?

We would all like to think things would be better if the teacher did her job. That would be nice. You would be able to come home after a long day's work and enjoy your child. Homework would be done, and you would be able to sit together and watch a show after having dinner and cleaning up together. But that situation seems like a lovely dream because it is so far removed from your reality. Yet, you dream of that day, as most of us do. You want to appreciate and be appreciated by your child.

This book will show you how to work with your child's teacher to help this dream of yours become a reality. You do want things to change for you and your family, don't you? Yes, you do—yet the tools you need seem so foreign that you are not sure where to start. Do not fear—this book will guide you, I promise. Let's begin by looking at some of the things you will learn in this book:

- **You will learn how to communicate with your child.** Listening creates strong family bonds that will help you connect. When your child feels truly heard, you will notice that many discipline problems will begin to disappear at home and at school.

- **You will teach your child gratitude by putting yourself first.** Yes! When you teach your child that you are important, he/she will begin to see you as important and will appreciate the sacrifices you make.

- **You will learn about the importance of routines and how they can become life habits to empower your child.** Once you learn to communicate with your child, you'll learn how to develop routines that your child will stick with, and that will turn into lifetime habits. Therefore, you will not have to worry about waking up to the nightmare you have been living, up until now.

- **You will discover how the skills you teach your child transfer to his/her good academic work.** When you begin modeling the skills of listening and helping your child to understand that you also matter, you truly begin to work as a team with your child's teacher. The ideas and dialogues you share with your child will begin to permeate class discussions and shape his/her own thoughts, ideas, and writing.

- **You will learn how thinking develops and how you can enrich your child's thinking by using the tools you already have.** Wow! That would be so nice. A better behaved child and grades going up—it can't get better than that. Yet it can and should.

- **You will learn how to work with your child's teacher as part of a team.** That is, ultimately, the goal of this book. We will learn how to work together rather than against each other as advocates for our mutual goal—what is best for your child.

Yes! This book will teach you how to accomplish all of these goals and maybe even more. Believe it or not, all these goals are achievable. You can do it with the right coaching. This book provides the insights and tools you need to help you become the parent you have always wanted to be.

You might be wondering, "Who is this person writing this book? How does she know about my struggles, and who is she to teach me how to solve some of them?" Well, I am and have been both a teacher and librarian for almost fifteen years. More importantly, I am the mother of a fifteen-year-old girl and a seventeen-year-old boy. I do not want my children to misbehave, but rather, to succeed in school and in life. I feel your pain and anxiety as you worry about your child's future. I see you or parents like you struggle every day with these problems. You come to me, at dismissal time, to ask how you can help your child. You do so when you think others are not watching because you are afraid they will judge you. Do not worry; those parents are struggling with the same problems. Please, know your secret is safe with me.

To think that your child will be judged by the behaviors he/she exhibits is scary. Will others like my child? Will others accept my child? These are questions we all ask ourselves. Yet, most likely, you find yourself paralyzed, not sure of how to help your child improve academically and, dare I say, behavior-wise. You are also afraid of being judged. Just remember—nobody is walking in your shoes; others can look and judge by what they see externally, but they are not walking in your shoes. The worst part is you are trying unsuccessfully and finding yourself going through the motions. You are paralyzed and find it so hard to move forward. How can you when you are not sure of how to improve things?

Do not worry. You are not alone, as I said previously; so many parents are fighting this same battle. However, I want to help you by coaching you through this difficult period. I have written this book because I know what you and so many other parents are going through. There is no need to see more parents and teachers struggling. We all want the same thing—success for our students and children. As a teacher, I will show you how we can work together. We truly can work together. Wouldn't it be nice to have someone to help you through this hard period? Remember, I spend many hours with your child (or students just like your child). I have grown to care for your child, and I see many of the behaviors that you see at home. If we work together, we can become a common front. United, we can guide your child to a better place. Think about my proposition; please do. We can achieve much more together, and up until now, what we have been doing has not been as successful as we would like. We have nothing to lose and much to gain. Please walk with me.

So are you ready? Are you ready to begin our journey? I promise the rewards are great. You will be able to help your child, and at the same time, be able to discover a new you. Come on; it is time teachers and parents united on this path we call education. Together, we can do this.

You are coming! Thank you! Thank you! I knew you would. Let's move on. It is time to get started.

Lovingly,
Your child's teacher
Dana M. Arias

LETTER 1

Learning Skills and Dinner — How They Connect

Dear Parents,

Now that school has ended and children are free to enjoy you and the summer, I want to ask you for help. Your help is important to prepare your children for next September. It will help them become a better student and adult. The help I need is very simple and many of you might already be doing it.

What I am asking is for you to sit down at dinner time with your children every night. You might wonder how this helps me, your child's teacher.

Well, it helps me on many levels. The first one is that it sets a routine your children can count on. This gives them the gift of stability. A child who feels secure is more likely to succeed in school.

The second way it helps is that your child will learn to stay on task. A child who has the habit of sitting down for dinner usually will not struggle as much when sitting in a classroom. This will permit him/her to focus and to not distract other students.

The third way this helps is that when you have dinner you will most likely converse with your child. When you converse, your child will learn to focus which will help him in the classroom. A child who can focus is more able to pay attention and tends to retain more of what is presented and discussed in the classroom. All children are required to participate in classroom conversations and are responsible for active exchanges of information. This skill is necessary at school and in every profession.

When you exchange information with your child, you have the great opportunity to see the world through your child's eyes. You can then encourage ideas and provide guidance or correct them if you believe they need correcting or loving encouragement.

Also, the exchange of ideas and stories dramatically increases your child's listening and speaking skills. We all know that those who express themselves with ease are most likely to be heard. What many parents do not realize is the ability to express ideas verbally translates to being able to express yourself in writing. You can only write down what you have thought and heard. The greater number of ideas you interchange with your child the more this will shape his/her thinking and writing.

This exchange will also give your child the opportunity to build background knowledge which is needed as a building block to learning new information. As a teacher my lesson on eco-systems is more successful if my students know what an ocean is. A unit on nutrition is more effective is students already know the names of different fruits and vegetable. Your daily conversations will help build a background that allows me to make meaningful connections in the classroom.

I wish you and your family a wonderful summer full of tasty dinners and great conversations!

Lovingly,
Your child's teacher

LETTER 2

Learning How to Listen

Dear Parents,

I was so touched by your question, "How do I get my child to talk to me about what really matters?" Great question!

One of the hardest things for most of us is establishing good conversational skills. This process takes a lot of time and patience. Listening and responding are skills that are learned and cultivated. The hardest part for most of us is learning to listen.

In a conversation, it is easy to think of answers when we are assuming we know what someone is going to say. Therefore, we do not really hear the other person's ideas. In reality, we are only listening to our thoughts and partially listening to the other person's words and ideas.

When conversing with your child, you truly need to listen. Listening means you are not giving advice, admonishing, or filling in the gaps. It means that you stop what you are doing and make eye contact with your child. You listen, nod, and, from time to time, paraphrase what you have heard. This response from you assures your child that you're engaged, interested, and are attentively following the conversation.

Please do not become discouraged when you start these new ways of listening—it is not easy to listen and to change! New habits take time and continuous practice because you are retraining yourself to become a better listener and conversationalist with your child. I truly applaud your hard work and dedication. You must love your child to be making the effort.

The next part is something of a challenge, but I know you will be able to do it. Remember to be kind to yourself as you are erasing old patterns you developed long ago. One of the new skills you need to develop is not to judge yourself or your child.

Your child is learning new ideas and behaviors. Believe me when I tell you she is doing the best she can. When she tells you that she hit Suzy or was made fun of, she is looking for guidance and support. Please do not jump to any conclusion. Instead, ask how she feels. "Why did you do that?" "Do you think that was correct?" "Why do you think it was correct or incorrect?" "How do you think the other person felt?"

All these questions will start a meaningful dialogue if you do not judge. If you do, because you also are learning, forgive yourself. You are entitled to make mistakes. Then analyze what you did do right and share it with your child. Tell her you realize you made a judgment and that you are working on becoming a better listener. More importantly, let your child know that you are trying to improve as a parent because you love him or her.

If you ever feel like you need to apologize, do so. You will never stop being amazed at how loving and forgiving your child is. Then continue to work on your listening skills and your ability to accept others. Becoming a proficient listener requires practice. With some patience and persistence, you will become a great listener. Remember, you can do it!

Lovingly,
Your child's teacher

LETTER 3

Encouraging as We Learn to Listen

Dear Parents,

Please do not become discouraged. Some of you have said you are trying to be better listeners, and yet your children will not talk or listen to you. How frustrating it all is! However, let me assure you that you are on the right path.

Even though this is a positive change, your child needs time to adjust. He might be thinking, "What is going on with Mom/Dad and the family? They normally preach. What is this about?" In many ways, any change is unsettling.

Think about it this way. You have a boss. This boss is always telling you what to do. If you mess up, you will not hear the end of it. One day, out of the blue, your boss goes to a seminar where he learns that he needs to have more meaningful dialogues with you to increase productivity. The next day, he puts all these new ideas into practice. You and your coworkers are surprised and not sure of things. Why the sudden change? What do they want? You think that there must be some negative reason for this new behavior.

In reality, your boss is just trying to keep his job by improving communications because they can lead to higher productivity. This situation is not all that different from your role as a parent. You want better communication with your child so you can have a better relationship and so he or she can succeed in school and life. Please keep these points in mind as you continue to work on your own ability to listen attentively and not judge.

If your children are out of sorts, you are on the right path! Even a negative response from them means they are noticing the changes in you and are trying to figure things out. They are probably thinking, "Where do I fit in all of this?" Be patient and keep up the good work. You are becoming a better listener. The key is to let them know that you are trying to improve as a parent and listener. As the days go by and your children see that you are honest in your efforts, they will respect you more and start confiding in you. Don't give up! You are on the right path.

Lovingly,
Your child's teacher

LETTER 4

Listening Creates Strong Family Bonds

Dear Parents,

Listening is so hard for many of us as life gets busier and busier. Many children and adults do not know how to listen. It is not a matter of hearing. Most of us hear perfectly well. Your children can hear perfectly well. The problem is that hearing is not the same as listening. How are they different?

Listening is a skill that needs to be developed. Listening means that, for a moment, we suspend what we are doing to hear—with our ears, our mind, and our heart—what others are saying. It requires an understanding of what the person is saying. Our full attention toward the other person is needed. More importantly, we have to see what the other person is saying behind the initial statement.

Let me give you an example. Your child says, "Mommy, I don't want to go to my friend's birthday party." Many parents might say that decision is fine and drop it. In other words "I heard it" and it is over with. However, if we look closely and listen, you will discover that your child not wanting to go to a birthday party might have something more behind it.

Did your child have an argument with the friend? Was your child not invited? Is your child feeling insecure or bothered by something? Maybe your child does not want you to spend money on a present because money is tight. There may be many reasons. The thing is that when we listen, we can get an insight into our child's world.

Without listening, we are clueless; we really do not see what is going on in our children's lives. Then we become surprised when our children get frustrated and upset. They tell us we don't listen. We say we are listening, but we are clueless because we really have not been listening. We are trying to figure out what the anger our child is directing at us is all about, and we truly don't know. The anger is at not being heard or understood.

Your child might not know how to express the following: "Mommy, I had an argument with Suzy because she said '____,' and now she said she does not want me to go to the party with her." So when we say, "That's fine," our children get upset because we are "not listening" to what they are feeling.

Not listening to the whole person does not only apply to our children. It also applies to our work, to our relationships with partners, spouses, friends, and family. Not listening is one of the biggest reasons why so many misunderstandings happen in our society. We are so busy going from A to Z that we do not stop to listen. What seems important to us loses value if we do not stop and listen.

So many of us try so hard to make sure our children have the best clothes, the best toys, and the latest gadget. We work very hard so our children have all of these things. This is how we show our children that we love and care for them. Yet, if we stop and listen, truly listen, we would know that our children would change all of that in exchange for special bonding time with us.

As an example, let me tell you a story from my childhood. When I was about sixteen years old, my father brought a man to our home. It turns out this man was the president of a major corporation in Mexico. my father and he were picking up some papers my father had left at home. I ran up to my dad and gave him a hug and a kiss and left. This behavior was very natural for me.

My dad's colleague saw my behavior and became very emotional. Later on, my dad told us what this man said to him after he witnessed my affection for my father. He had worked all of his life to give his children everything they needed and wanted. They did not want for any material goods, but his kids were not happy. They were studying at one of Mexico's best universities, and even though they lived in the same house, his house was empty. His wife was out and about, the kids did their things, and he arrived every evening to a house, not a home. They had everything—houses, cars, clothes, trips, etc. What was missing?

This father and his children were missing the bonds that come from listening. They were missing the ties that are strengthened when we understand what the other person is saying and develop empathy for him. Listening is the glue that helps us grow and develop into caring people. These are the bonds that show someone "I love you."

Perhaps we do not value this skill anymore because we do not see it as something tangible like a toy or a game. Yet its value, to us and our children, is priceless because it will build our family unity. It is the cement that brings families together. It is what will make your children be there for you when you are old because you valued them when they were young and throughout their lives.

If you need to start listening to your child, do so. Even if it is out of pure selfishness because you do not want to end up like the man who came to my home, listen to your child. This individual act of selfishness might end up being the best gift you give yourself, your children, and your family.

Lovingly,
Your child's teacher

LETTER 5

Listening to Our Own Needs Actually Benefits the Family

Dear Parents,

You say you don't know how to start. You say you don't know how to tell your child that you are trying to listen. You say you are frustrated because nobody is listening to you, and now you have to listen to someone else when you are hurting. You are doing the best you can and you just don't know what else you can do.

You want things to go well, and you are so overwhelmed because you are trying and just don't seem to be making much headway. You feel lonely with this burden you are carrying. Somehow, life has taken over and you find yourself lost and lonely. How can you help your children when you yourself are aching? How can you make things right?

Start by listening to yourself. What is it that you need? Do you need to sleep? Do you need to cry? Do you need to shout? Do you need to vent? What is it that you need? What do you need to help yourself feel better? Stop and think about it. Truly stop and let yourself feel what it is that you need.

Why is it so important that you understand your own needs? Because if you do not understand yourself first, you cannot help your children and family in the way they need. Your best efforts will fall short because you are hurting as well. No matter what your intentions, the pain and hurt of not having your needs met will permeate everything you do.

Sometimes, we kid ourselves and think our needs do not matter, but they do. If we are tired and have not slept, we will snap at our children when we get frustrated with them. Are we being mean? No, we are being human. However, let me be clear; our humanness does not serve as an excuse for NOT doing what is right. If we are so tired, we should go get some sleep.

We should not be running around doing errands and barking at our kids because we are tired. Believe me; it is better that the child misses a play date or a class because you took a nap than that you take your child to the class or play date and have a miserable time with him or her in the car. Some of us can't even take a nap because we don't have someone to babysit. It is time to slow down. The dishes in the sink can wait. It is preferable to take care of our needs and not run the risk of becoming upset and snapping. At these times, we say something that unintentionally can hurt our children's feelings; then we end up feeling miserable because we hurt their feelings.

We need to realize that we matter. What we do to help ourselves become more grounded will also help our families and, ultimately, ourselves in all aspects of our lives. As heads of our homes, we need to be well. When the head of the home falls apart, most likely the rest of the family will struggle. So ask yourself: What do I need to be okay?

Sometimes, the answer to this question will be an easy one. I need to eat. I need to sit quietly for a few minutes. Other times, the answer you are seeking will be elusive. We know we need something, but we are not sure what it is. Try to sit and listen to what your heart is telling you. The answer will come to you. Maybe not immediately, but it will come. Observe your surroundings and listen. It will come.

Your body is great at telling you what you need. You just need to observe it. At first, you might need help to understand it. When you get sick, the actual part of your body that is ill, at that time, is trying to tell you what you need to look at. Do so. Pay attention to your body because it is giving you great clues about what you need to work at. Listening to your body and spirit will give you great insight into what you need to be well. Then act on what it tells you. Do whatever you need to do to help yourself and your family.

You are your family's backbone. Your family members' wellbeing depends on your wellbeing. Take care of yourself; pamper and love yourself because you are important and you matter. The problem is that many of us get caught up in our obligations and responsibilities and forget about ourselves. Let's not forget: We are the pillar that holds our family together.

The better we are at meeting our own needs, the better we will be at meeting our family's needs. Remember, we can't give what we don't have. Being complete will always help us to help our families. In many ways, taking care of ourselves first can feel like a selfish way to act, but it is a necessary one. We need to make sure we are well so we can be there for our families so they will be okay. Let's indulge ourselves in this little bit of selfishness.

Lovingly,
Your child's teacher

LETTER 6

Taking Care of You Is Not Selfish! It Is Necessary

Dear Parents,

Some of you were surprised by my last letter. You think that parents should be generous with their children. I agree that we should be generous with our children. But we can't be generous with our children if we are not generous with ourselves. Think about it for a moment.

When you are feeling well, happy, and full of life, you are in a position to share. Giving becomes easy when we are emotionally well. Now, think of it in a different light. You are not feeling well; you are overworked and tired. Your child comes and asks you to take him to the mall. You don't want to go because you need to rest for a while. Yet you might do it because it is what a "good parent" does. But is it done with a good disposition? Do you do it out of love or a sense of duty? Do you do it just to quiet your child and get him out of the way?

Many times we do things because we believe it is a "should do," a "must do," or a "need to do." When we follow these "shoulds, needs, and musts," we are not being true to ourselves—true to the most important person in our life. Yes, the most important person in your life is you! We forget this fact, and we don't speak of it because people might consider us selfish. But don't forget that you need to consider yourself; your needs have to be met in order for you to be a good parent. It is not selfish to say, "I need to take a nap. I will help you as soon as I am rested."

Please think about this: YOU ARE IMPORTANT! YOU DO MATTER! Do not let anybody tell you any differently. Take care of yourself and rediscover what an amazing person you are. Your children will love that incredible person, too!

Lovingly,
Your child's teacher

LETTER 7

Putting Parents' True Needs First Can Teach Gratitude

Dear Parents,

    I don't know how many times I have heard the "selfless parent" cry: "I am such a good mother/father/parent because I put my children first." "I will not sleep because I need to stay next to my child." "I will sit here and beg my child to eat." "I have been driving all afternoon so my kids can enjoy soccer, ballet, and singing." "I just don't know why after I have sacrificed for my child the way I have, my child is so ungrateful."

    The reason why your children do not appreciate what you do for them is because you did not put yourself first. You taught them, since they were young, that you do not count and they do. You are the all-sacrificing parent because your child is worth all of the sacrifice in the world—even if it means that you put yourself and your needs last. But there is a difference between sacrificing and becoming somebody's doormat. Without realizing it, we become our children's doormats.

    Our children do not realize this because they don't know any other way of being. They have always worked within this model.

If they need something, it is given to them without any hesitation. So they do not know how to give appreciation. Even when we ask them to say thank you, they don't get it. They truly do not see the sacrifice and effort we are putting into their wellbeing. As with all things, appreciation is something that needs to be taught.

We start by teaching our children that "we count." Our children need to understand that we have a responsibility toward them, yet the way we do things for them is a choice. We have to feed and clothe and provide a roof for them. We are responsible for providing an education for them as well. Yet we do not have to provide the best of everything for them. That is a choice we make out of love.

We choose to sacrifice and take that extra job so our children can have the toy they desire for the holiday. We choose not to buy the jacket we really want so we can pay for the expensive shoes our child wants, not needs. We make these choices. Yes, we make them out of a sense of love. Yet, we never tell our children we are making them. Our children have no idea of our sacrifices because we don't tell them. Therefore, they have a huge sense of entitlement rather than a sense of gratitude.

We need to explain to them that many of the things we do are done out of love for them. If they don't understand that, then we need to teach them gratitude. Thankfulness can't and won't come to our children if we do not make them aware of how lucky they are to have all they have.

As parents, we need to teach our children that "we count." Our feelings and our needs also need to be met in order for us to be able to give out of joy and not a sense of duty. When we teach our children that we also count, we are sending two powerful messages to them. First, "I am important and what I do is done for you because I love you." Second, we teach them how they are to treat others as well as how to treat us when we get old. If we continue to give to our children without setting limits, they will only feel entitlement and very little gratitude. They will become selfish and self-centered.

In a family, all individuals are expected to give and share. When we teach our children these expectations, we will start to feel heard as well, and communicating with our children will be much easier. Now the effort is not only yours; your child will have to become invested in communicating with you and appreciating you.

Lovingly,
Your child's teacher

LETTER 8

Teaching Our Children Values Through Small Moments

Dear Parents,

Yes, parenthood is hard. It certainly isn't easy. We can only do our best and hope that we are doing things well. Please don't get discouraged. You are doing the best you can, and that is all you can do. Keep that in mind. Reading and learning other ways of being a better parent is already a huge step.

The fact that you are trying speaks volumes. And yes, you are right; many things we do are because we see them in the media. Yes, we also think that the media will have the answer for us—sometimes it does; sometimes it doesn't. It is up to us to see what the media is trying to "sell" to us.

I am not talking about products; I am talking about ideas. The media sells big and little ideas. As a matter of fact, they sell all types of ideas, such as: "It's good to be thin" or "If you buy a certain product, you will become extremely attractive." These are the ideas I am talking about. However, it is up to us to stop and think about them. "Are they for me? Why? Why not? Do I want my child to grow up with those images and ideas?" We need to think about the concepts we teach our children. We need to ask ourselves, "What are we teaching them?" and "What are we letting the media teach them?"

If we never have time to listen to our children, and we only give the material things, we are somehow failing. Let me give you an example: Years ago, I was at a very elegant party. There were waiters, cocktails, the works. It was quite impressive. At some point during the party, the host unveiled a very expensive car as his son's birthday present. The son said, "Thank you" and left. Later, as the young man was talking with his friends, he said, "Another present to show off to his friends." I was much younger and I did not get it. Now I do. The young man thought his father had bought him the present so his father could say, "I can afford this for my son." What the father's true intentions were will always be a mystery to me. What is not a mystery is what the son really wanted. He wanted and needed his father's loving attention. Yet his father was so wrapped up in his own needs that he could not see what his son was wanting.

At times, we are blinded by what we see and by what we are told are the right ways. We forget then to ask in our heart what we really need to do. We forget to be still and observe our surroundings. What makes us happy? What makes those we love happy? Is it material things? Yes, we all want "things." But what makes us really happy? In reality, they are the simple things. Let me share with you what are some of my daily happy moments.

One of my biggest daily highlights is having breakfast with my daughter. I get up every morning (Monday through Friday)—no matter how tired I am—to make breakfast. The table will be set with placemats, juice, and coffee, and we enjoy twenty minutes for ourselves. Our conversations are great ones. When I leave for work, I am left with a sense of gratitude and love for my daughter. She is left with a full belly and a sense that she is important to her mother. I have not given her any material gift. Yet I have given her the richest gift I can give—time. The undivided time and attention I have invested in her, show her the deep love I have for her. She knows she means the world to me.

Now, I have to be truthful with you. I have always known that having breakfast with my daughter is important and I have done it as much as I can. Then, I slipped. Life caught up with me and I stopped doing it. Things were fine, but I was missing something and I was not sure what it was. I received a clue from Marcus Buckingham's book *Find Your Strongest Life*. It showed me the way back. Throughout the book, Buckingham shows us that we need to look for those moments that make us full and powerful; he tells us to look carefully into the small details of our lives, and in them, we will find what makes us strong and happy. Once we discover them, we need to find ways to recreate them every day. By doing so, we will grow powerful within ourselves. What a lesson!

When I realized that one of the things I loved most was spending time with my daughter, I actively started to create opportunities to spend time with her. It has meant that I don't talk half as much on the phone as I used to. It means I screen calls. It means I have become more selective of whom I give my time to. You can call me selfish, but I would not change it for the world. We, as parents, need to see to whom we are giving our time. Why do we give our time to all those other people who are not our family? Is it necessary to give so much to others and take away from those whom we truly love? What needs within ourselves are we trying to fulfill when we devote so much time to outside interests and not to our children? These are some of the questions we need to ask ourselves.

When we find these answers, we will be ready to listen better to ourselves and our children. Then we won't have to buy an expensive car to show our children that we love them. Our love for them will flow through in so many other ways that are fulfilling to us and our loved ones—in other words, our family.

Thank you for listening to my thoughts. Please know I have tried to listen with an open heart to your comments. I hope I have understood what you are trying to tell me and, more importantly, I am providing you with my own valuable insight.

Lovingly,
Your child's teacher

LETTER 9

Learning to Self-Regulate and Communicate

Dear Parents,

As parents, we sometimes forget to carve out some time for ourselves. We consider everybody else's needs but forget our own. Paying attention to what we require to be healthy and happy individuals is important. When we do pay attention to what we need, we teach our children a wonderful lesson. We teach them to self-regulate, which means that they learn to listen to what their hearts, bodies, minds, and souls need. As they pay attention to what those internal feelings are saying to them, they will learn to understand themselves and become cognizant of what truly matters in their lives.

How do we teach this difficult skill, which most of us have not mastered? We teach it by modeling the behavior we want our children to emulate. We begin by listening to ourselves—something that is hard for most of us because we are so accustomed to being on autopilot.

We run from one place to another, hoping we have enough hours in the day to get everything we need done. We will not eat a proper meal because we have to run, run, run. We do not stop to collect our thoughts because we have so much to do. We do not take a much-needed nap because the dishes need to be done. All these things we have to do are important, but it is more important to teach our children how to take care of themselves in the same way that we show them we take care of ourselves.

When we stop to take a much-needed rest and tell our children, "I will watch you play, but first, I need to sit and be quiet right now," we are teaching them two things: 1) We consider ourselves important, and 2) We are capable of taking care of ourselves. We don't need someone else to make us feel well or good about who we are. In other words, we are modeling the behavior we want. We are telling our child, "I am capable of listening to what I need and making sure I get those necessities met."

When we do stop to meet our own needs, we need to say to our children what we are doing and why. The dialogue we present them with will be the one they will begin to emulate in their own minds. "I am tired; I have run around, but now I need to sit." This example seems simple, but it is very powerful because we want our children to listen to themselves, to what their own inner voices are saying.

It is necessary for our children to understand and listen to that little voice because it can guide them to a better place. Remember Pinocchio? He did not listen very well to that little inner voice, did he? Listening to our own inner voice is important. When we do so, we normally find ourselves in a better place, and when we are in a better place, we find it easier to communicate our needs and ideas to others, which brings me to the way I have witnessed children communicate.

I have witnessed three ways that children express themselves. Let me explain them, so it is easier for you to understand what your child is trying to tell you:

1. Stating what they want directly. What they say is like an arrow that goes from point A to point B. "I want a chocolate." No mystery there; we know what they want.

2. Going around in circles when explaining something. The explanation seems to spiral from one thing to another and does not appear to be very cohesive. Please understand that what your children are doing is trying to make sense of something. They don't have a full grasp of what they are trying to understand, and as they are speaking, they are piecing it together.

So we need to be patient. They truly are making an effort to understand what they are thinking. They have to bring many different concepts together into a simple cohesive idea. This process is not easy; many adults also struggle with putting ideas together. Watch carefully for the "ums" and "hmms" your children say as they struggle to make sense of what they are expressing. It is not that these children are not capable of thinking; it is that they are trying to piece together something into a cohesive whole.

We need to let our children explain and to help them through the process. Let's not hurry them. Being patient with them is often where we are challenged because it can be very frustrating to wait, especially if we have a lot of things to do. The only way to get better at putting our ideas together into a cohesive unit is through practice. Shouldn't we let our children practice with us?

3. Jumping from one subject to another. In many ways, this explanation seems obvious and similar to the second one I described above, except in this case, children don't stop talking. Listening to them is like changing stations on the radio. These children normally seem to think much faster than their mouths can go. Articulating their ideas is not much of a problem. It is obvious they have many ideas and opinions. Listening to them is overwhelming at times because they have so much to say and they jump from one topic to another, not making much sense at all. Yet their ideas are good. They need to be given a sounding block (you and me) who listens to them and helps put their thoughts in order.

You will recognize this type of communication when you see children who are very excited. These children need to be reminded to slow down and think of what it is they want to say. We, as adults, need to help them put their thoughts in order so they can learn how to communicate successfully. Again, this process takes patience—a lot of patience on our part. But if we succeed at being patient and helping our children put their ideas in order, we truly help each one to communicate his or her needs and thoughts to him- or herself (the main character in that child's life). By listening and helping them organize their thoughts, we can help our children begin to understand what they need to self-regulate. This process is challenging for them and for us as listeners, yet it needs to be done. (These ideas tie into our children's writing, which I will explain in another letter).

My hope is for you to figure out which of these three ways best describes how your child expresses him- or herself; once you understand your child's process of expression, it will make listening to your child easier for you. Remember, what I have described here is based on my observing and listening to children. If you watch your child closely, you will also be able to pick up on these communication patterns.

As always, thank you for listening.
Lovingly,
Your child's teacher

LETTER 10

Connecting Our Ideas and Oral Language to Writing is the Key to Success

Dear Parents,

You asked me how I came up with the three types of communication I described in the last letter. I observed your children. I paid attention to what they said and how they said it. It was important to me because the way we speak says a lot about how we are thinking and processing our ideas. As a teacher, my main goal is to create thinkers and future contributors to society.

As a teacher of writing, I have noticed that the majority of my students have a very hard time communicating their ideas. At first, I thought this issue resulted from the process of their writing down their ideas; after all, writing is a difficult skill to master. So, I kept trying all the different ideas and techniques I knew that could help them, but I still was not making much progress. I was so frustrated that I truly began to think something was wrong with me as a teacher. At the time, I was taking a course on how to help gifted children succeed, and the professor said something that has always stuck with me, "We write as we speak." WOW! The following Monday, I was listening to my students. I mean it; I was listening to them talk. I paid attention as they spoke to each other at recess, in lunch, or in the classroom, but especially, how they spoke and interacted with their parents at pick-up time and any other time I could listen. I went as far as listening to parents talk with their children when I was in the grocery store.

Unfortunately, not much was being said. Parents were normally on the phone and grabbing groceries while the kids talked to each other or played electronic games or nagged their parents in order to get some type of attention. Every once in awhile, I saw a parent talking to his or her child, and then my heart sang with joy.

I realized that most of my students had a hard time expressing their ideas. Many could not answer a "why" question comfortably. They truly struggled and became frustrated. Instead, they goofed off and joked around or became quiet. The ones who did not answer most likely were afraid of making a mistake and proving themselves to be vulnerable. The jokers would talk nonsense to give themselves enough room to back down if they had to. In many ways, this situation reminded me of a study I had read years ago about the way women communicate. Many women will say something like "I think this might be important because…." It's important here that they would say, "I think" because if confronted and challenged, it gave them an option to back down. Many of my students also had created ways to back down and not express what they thought. I was so sad to make this discovery that I realized I needed to create a way for them to express themselves.

My students' oral communication was affecting their writing skills. So I began to listen, and that is when I observed the patterns I described before. These observations have become one of the main motivators of these letters and this book.

Please know that I care deeply for your children; after all, they are mine for a good part of the day. As I get to know them individually, I see their personalities and I can't avoid loving them. I believe most teachers feel the same way about their students. But I also believe I speak for most teachers when I say this: We teachers can't do it all.

We only have limited time with your children, and much of that time is occupied by teaching and practicing with several students. Part of the time is also occupied with administrative duties we need to complete according to state and school requirements. To help your children succeed academically, we need your help. Will you help us by conversing with them more? It is so necessary.

As you speak more with your children, sentences will become longer and more cohesive. Your children's ideas will be clearer to themselves and others. They will share their ideas and be able to bounce them off of you, allowing them to create stronger points of view. They will be able to hear themselves think, and they will begin to embellish those ideas and thoughts. They will become aware of their own thinking and know they have something of value to say. They will know they are capable of contributing to themselves, their families, their communities, their country, and most importantly to our wonderful world. They will know they can make a difference.

Please help us help your child.
Lovingly,
Your child's teacher

LETTER 11

Writing Helps Clear Our Thoughts

Dear Parents,

I understand that some questions came to your mind when you read the previous letter. However, the main one was how conversing and writing are interrelated. You have asked such a good and complex question. Thank you for asking. Let me try to answer it with a personal anecdote.

A few years ago, I met Dr. Wayne Dyer. He had just finished a presentation and a few people approached him for autographs. I was one of them. I was lucky enough to ask him how I could fulfill my dream of becoming a public speaker like he was. He looked at me and said he did not know. Then, as an afterthought, Dr. Dyer said I needed to write because it would help me to clear my thoughts.

I was not sure of his advice because I am dyslexic and writing is such a hard task for me. But as I thought about it, I realized that he was right. My thoughts were scattered everywhere. My brain normally rushed from one thought to another, never finishing or completing an idea. This chaos was apparent in the way I spoke. I spoke about a thousand words a minute and barely stopped to breathe. How could I ask someone to follow my patterns of thought if I had no idea what my thoughts were half the time?

As always, when there is a need and a desire to improve, teachers will show up—in this case, they were my dear friends. They would listen to me and interject small ideas or phrases into my ramblings, forcing me to stop and think about what I was saying. It was not that my ideas were bad or wrong; it was just that they were not clear. They needed to be defined and clarified. My speech patterns became different now because I was truly trying to improve as a teacher and as a writer.

I was listening to what my friends said. Their thoughts and questions were important because they held keys to what they understood from my ramblings. In other words, was I expressing my ideas clearly? How clearly? What needed clarifying and why? Had I gotten to the central point, or had I gone around in circles, not truly addressing the topic but thinking I was? All these questions and many more became such an important part of my discourse with my friends. I needed their input to help me become clear in my thinking. Let me tell you that being clear when I think and speak is something I still work at; we all do. Most of us need to hear ourselves speak to understand whether what we are saying is clear. Let me give you an everyday example:

I say to my husband and children, "I am not happy with how you are picking up the bathroom after you shower." I am sure that what I said was clear.

Yet, they say that it is clean. As far as they are concerned, the towels are picked up and there are no clothes on the floor. This is their definition of cleanliness. When they ask me why I think it is not clean, I am able to discuss it with them. Because we do not share the same definition of cleanliness, I have to define my definition for them. So I need to proceed and let them know that they need to wipe off the sink, pick up all the hairs from the floor, and put the top on the toothpaste besides picking up the towels and dirty clothes. These interactions are the ones that help ideas be clear. Defining things and being specific brings clarity to my mind and, hopefully, some peace of mind to them. Yet if I don't say it out loud, most likely I will mull it over a thousand times in my head, unsure whether or not there was clarity in what I need so we can all enjoy a clean bathroom. Becoming aware of this lack of communication in what we say and what we mean is key to understanding each other.

We all perceive that we speak clearly. But do we?

All of these small discussions and conversations help us become better thinkers because we are interchanging ideas and different perceptions. It is not important here whether we are correct or wrong in the given situation. What matters is that we are expressing ourselves and backing up our ideas. In other words, we are thinking and producing new thoughts.

Now, how does this need for clarity in our thoughts and speech influence or affect our writing? Hugely! We can't write down what we have not thought. Our writing becomes a mirror of what is going on in our brains. Did I understand the concept? What did I not understand? Did I reflect what I understood? All of these are questions and answers that will be expressed in our writing. We need to put our thoughts in order so we are able to express our ideas. It is that simple. Yet many of us struggle with writing because it is one of the harder skills we learn at school, and we do not have the opportunity to bounce ideas off each other.

Most teachers I know (I am lucky to work with some incredible teachers) teach and model how to think of ideas in clearer ways. But again, we are in need of your help. When you discuss ideas and concepts with your children, you help them grow and practice what we modeled. You help them bring clarity to their thoughts. The next day, they come back to school with new ideas and they challenge their classmates with these new points of view. Suddenly, our classrooms are alive because the children realize they have something to say. THEY HAVE A VOICE! Yes, a voice and many cool and interesting ideas to go with it. At this point, they are ready to start thinking about writing.

Now, I am going to let you think about this topic. Please create your own ideas about what has been said about the relationship between thoughts, speech, and writing. Make your own conclusions because how you treat this topic will be the guiding force behind your child's thoughts.

I promise the next letter will be about how we as teachers use this new powerful voice your child is discovering. Yes, we will apply all of this information to writing.

As always, I have so much respect and gratitude for you. Thank you for listening and becoming my ally in the academic education of your child.

Lovingly,
Your child's teacher

LETTER 12

Writing Helps Us Discover Our Voice

Dear Parents,

As promised, I will do my best to explain the relationship between conversing with our children and writing.

Writing is a complex skill that is formed from many individual components. The development of each one is important for a child to be a strong writer. Yet the key ingredient is believing we have something important to say. When we discover our own voice, we have opened a magic box of unlimited possibilities—we have discovered our ability to think and say what we think. More importantly, we realize that what we have to say is important and can influence others.

Remember, big ideas can change the world, but it is the small ideas that transform it. These small ideas show up as individual thoughts, but if nurtured, their possibilities are endless. Please think of Gandhi. Rather than create a violent revolution to free India from British rule, he decided to find another solution. His peaceful marches started as a small idea. Most people must have doubted they could succeed at first, yet his "small idea" prevailed and has transformed the world.

This same principle applies to your children. When they are conversing with you, they are explaining what they think and why they think it. You are, in many ways, the one who waters the ideas that are sprouting in their minds. If you stop and ask why they think something, you will be pleasantly surprised to find they can be pretty logical. Let me give you an example that is dear to my heart.

When I was reading the Harry Potter series, my daughter asked me to read it to her. She was only four years old, so I didn't think she would listen, but I decided to read the books to her anyway. I truly thought she would get tired and not listen. Was I wrong! She would sit and play on the rug, while I read out loud. When I would stop, she would ask me to continue. So I did.

We started discussing the plots of the books and their characters. She was creating her own theories about what was going to happen next. In other words, she was predicting. Many of her predictions were correct while others were not. Yet she was thinking, and this led her to writing. How could this be? After all, she was just learning her letters. Well, very simply, she started drawing her predictions. She would draw what she thought would happen and explain it to me.

Now, you can say that drawing is not writing, but it is its first precursor. Ask a child to tell you what the picture is all about. You can get a full story out of some simple scribbles. Yet to the child, they are so much more than scribbles. That is why I say that drawing is the precursor to writing. It is the way we all begin to communicate our written ideas. In many ways, it is the concrete way we can grab an abstract concept and make it visible to all. Therefore, drawing is writing, and as such, we should applaud our children's efforts. Those efforts are important and our children need to know that. Our response to their initial efforts will support and encourage them or will make them wilt. Our words and our encouragement are what make the difference in most cases.

You must wonder: What is the teacher's role in all of this? Well, the teacher helps the child's newfound voice develop in two ways. The first way is by continuing to expand on what has already been established at home. Teachers will present ideas and concepts that are meant to have the child think, explore, and expand upon what he or she already knows.

As the exploration continues, the children begin to learn critical thinking skills. I want to clarify this point because often we wonder how learning about a subject such as World War II will contribute to our child's life. It might or might not. What the teacher is getting at by teaching such subjects is the child's critical thinking skills. Critical thinking is not easy to teach, but it is extremely necessary if we want to create individuals who are capable of navigating through life.

Think of the movie *The Blind Side*, about a young man who eventually plays for the NFL. As he is learning to express his own thoughts and ideas, he finds himself struggling and in need of a tutor to help him succeed at school. There is a moment in the movie when the tutor is trying to help her student pick a topic to write about for an essay that will determine whether or not he graduates. She gives him several options, but none of them seem to spark much interest. Yet, when she gets the father involved in the discussion, there is a connection. The father relates and connects the reading and writing assignment to football and the assignment comes to life. Here is a connection of ideas, and suddenly, the battles in a battlefield are similar to those he faces on the football field, and the student is able to write an essay in which the ideas show an understanding of what was being said. Not only that, he is able to relate to the topic on a personal level.

When a personal connection is made, we are using higher order thinking skills. Once the connection is done, we begin to think in abstract terms and create our own concepts. We begin to challenge what is already known and thought of as a truth. At this point, we begin to question what is being presented to us, be it by our elders, a famous person, a politician, and even the media. More importantly, it needs to happen if we want to create thinkers and problem-solvers who are strong contributors to our society.

I want you to think about what I just explained. Think about it and come up with your own ideas. If need be, challenge me. I will not be offended. To the contrary, I will know I have succeeded because I have gotten you thinking. Having you think about this process of communication is important because your thoughts will create within you a conviction to help your children. That conviction will hopefully move you in the direction that we (the teachers) need help in: getting your children to connect with ideas and concepts.

I am aware that I told you there are two ways teachers play into how we teach your child writing. The first one is helping the students express their ideas. In other words, how do they process what they have learned and explain it orally? Remember, we write what we know. I will explain the second one in the following letters. For now, I will let you think about all that has been said.

As always, I can't thank you enough for listening to me. I hope that in these letters, you find a true guide.

Lovingly,
Your child's teacher

LETTER 13

Thinking Levels: How Do We Develop Them?

Dear Parents,

Before I move on to the second way teachers help your children's writing, I want to talk to you about the thinking skills we are helping our children develop. I am hoping I can paint a clear picture that will help you understand where your sons or daughters are in their thinking. Understanding their current thought level is a very powerful tool. It allows us to see what we need to do to help our children and students move forward in their thinking.

The best way for me to explain this point is by using an example. Yesterday, I was talking to one of my students about what was important to him. He mentioned several things that he considered important. His football, his house, and his parents were among the things he cared about. What he did during our conversation was very simple. He was recalling information.

Recalling information is not such a hard skill. We tried to remember a list, an event, some details, and we are able to recall them as part of what we know or have learned. All of us constantly recall information. It is a simple skill that comes naturally; even if we don't realize it at the time, it's there.

As we conversed, I asked my student why these things were important to him. His answers were heartwarming and full of understanding. He believed that his parents supported him throughout a hard time in his life. They showed their support by helping him prepare for the standardized test all children in the state of Illinois are required to take. His statement seems like a very simple one. Yet, it is full of understanding and comprehension. He was able to comprehend how important he was to his parents. Here again, the skill is a simple one.

We first recall information and try to comprehend it. We do this all the time. Understanding is important to all of us. Many a time we are stuck because we are not able to comprehend someone's intentions or motives. Once we understand, we are free to move on. So comprehension is a skill that goes above recalling information.

The next question I asked him was why he thought he was important to his parents. He began to think about this question. He began to describe different events in his life and try to understand why his parents did certain things for him. As he thought about what his parents did for him, he began to see that these events were also done for his brothers and sister. Therefore, his parents' ideas and behaviors were not exclusively directed at him. Why was it that they also applied these behaviors to others in his family?

This questioning process is important because many times we know and understand something, yet we need to see that it applies to more than one situation. These ideas can be transferred to others.

In other words, we can apply these ideas to other circumstances. In his case, he realized he was being treated as his siblings were.

Our conversation continued. We began to focus on why he was treated similarly to his siblings. Why was it that his parents expected him and his siblings to study? As he analyzed a bit more, he realized that his parents must really love his brothers, his sister, and him. What a powerful realization! As he told me about this realization, his eyes sparkled.

He had come to a new knowing. He had discovered something magical. Yes, he had always known that his parents loved him. The difference is that now he really knew what it meant. Initially, his words were simple: "My mom and dad love me." Now there was a *knowing* that nobody could take away from him. When we analyze, our understanding deepens, as you can see in my student's thinking.

My next question for him was why he thought his parents loved him. His immediate answer was "Well, they are my mom and dad." But I said to him, "I know that and so do you. My question is why do you think they love you?" He was not sure about this. So, I guided him again by asking, "What do you think your mom and dad like about you?" He began to list some ideas of why his parents loved him. We looked at them and tried to decide whether they were true or not. Was this right or not?

In the end, he decided that his parents loved him because they had always wanted a boy just like him. He was beaming! Now please think about this process; he had to put ALL the concepts together and synthesize them. What did he know? How did he know it? How did that make him feel? These were some of the questions that were coming together for him. The picture that was forming in his brain was a very powerful one. It was way beyond knowing "My parents love me."

The only thing we did not do was judge his parents' love. One can't judge the love a parent has for his or her child. My student was happy and that was all that mattered. However, if we wanted to go further with our thinking abilities, we would have had to evaluate the love his parents felt for him. Was it real love? Of course it was! There was no need to think further in this case. Sometimes, it is important to stop thinking and just embrace our new discoveries. This is the best part of a discovery—sitting back and savoring the new information.

As you can see with this example, I took you through the gamut of thinking. Thinking is not a simple process. Each one of its steps builds on the previous one. Sometimes, these steps get intertwined because thinking is not easy or simple. We have to train ourselves to work through the process. One of the best ways to do so is to guide your children's thinking by conversing with them. Having them answer simple questions such as "Who? What? When? Where? Why? and How?" is a great step toward achieving this goal. When we converse with our children, we are truly guiding their thinking.

Thank you for thinking about this topic. I know we, as teachers, will be able to count on your help.

Lovingly,
Your child's teacher

LETTER 14

Building New Ideas:
As We Learn and Think

Dear Parents,

In the previous letter, I spoke about how thinking builds upon itself. There is a sequence of steps that we follow as we think. We scaffold our thoughts. As I explain to my students, "We make magic when we think." Just imagine that! We take ideas and mix them. The magic is that we have created a new idea, and if we act on it by writing or making it become reality, the magic is even bigger. Well, this process has an academic component as well. The following example should help make it clear.

Let's say your child is learning how to read. The first skill your child will learn is to recognize the letters in the alphabet. The result of this process is that your child will look at a letter and be able to recall its name. When your child recalls the letter's name, he is showing his knowledge. The thing he knows is the name of the letter. The letter "A" is named the letter "A." So when children sing "The ABC Song," they show us they know a song, but not necessarily the letters. Many of them still don't recognize the individual letters and need to be taught what they look like. This knowledge will come in time.

The next step in our thinking scaffold is comprehension. We see how reading skills develop as our children learn that each letter has a sound that is unique to it. So our children move up in their thinking skills because they are able to comprehend that letters have a unique sound to them.

What follows is applying what has been learned by recognizing letters and their sounds to blend them and form simple words. Applying what we learn is not always simple. It requires us to focus and be engaged in what we are doing. Through hours of practice, we will be able to do so automatically, but again, it will be after many hours of practice. I say this because the majority of teachers need you to help your children practice reading.

If your child is struggling to "blend sounds together," it means he or she is still decoding; This means he is learning to put all the sounds together, and most likely there is no comprehension or very little of it. Children will need many hours of practice to improve their fluency, which comes after they have learned to decode words and letters. Once they become fluid readers, they can actually focus on the meaning of the text and are finally reading. There is no reading if there is no comprehension, even if they are sounding the words beautifully. To achieve true reading, your child most likely will need one-on-one practice. This practice can only be adequately given to children at home with their greatest teacher—you! Sit with them and have them read to you. Again, we teachers will teach the skill, but due to the limited time we have and the large amount of curriculum we must cover, we need your help. You do make a huge difference when you have your child practice the skills that were taught in school. Practice is what makes the difference in any of the skills that we teach. Remember, true reading is when we understand what is being read—not just sounding out the words and reading fluently. If there is no comprehension, there is no reading because reading is the transferring of ideas.

So the next step, after seeing that children are fluent at decoding the words on the page, is to ask ourselves, "Does my child understand what is being said in the sentence, paragraph, chapter, and or book?" If the answer is "No," your child is not reading; he or she is only decoding. It does not matter how fast your child decodes; if there is no comprehension of what is said, he or she is not reading.

You see, reading is picking up ideas from a written form; without the transfer of concepts, we are not reading. It is that simple. When we concentrate and focus on the ideas the author presents, we begin to analyze and make connections. Some connections will be simple. "The boy in the book is like me." Other ideas might be a bit more complex. "Wow, we are not that different from the children in China." You get the point: We are constantly analyzing as we read.

The next step is to synthesize—to put together everything we know. This step includes what we talked about at dinnertime, what we saw and heard on TV, maybe what we overheard at the grocery store, or read. All of these ideas that we pick up are discussed with our classmates and peers. We need to put all of these ideas together to create our own ideas. When we do, our perspectives will begin to change. What we thought was one way now appears to be a bit more complex. Other people see the situation differently—why? Am I right or are they? We realize we might both see it from a different perspective; we must then accept that there is not always only one way. There are many ways to look at what surrounds us. Accepting and looking at these different viewpoints helps us to become better thinkers. Teaching this concept to children is hard. It requires a lot of patience and dialogue. It is important to teach it because it is the beginning of teaching tolerance to ourselves and others.

These questions take us to our last step in the thinking process: We judge what we have learned. Evaluating is important to the thinking process because it helps us make decisions. When we consider two or more different points of view, we are reaffirming or challenging what we believe because, ultimately, we are going to judge based on our experiences. Let's use a historical scenario as an example.

Throughout the years, let's assume that we have heard that a certain group of people was "our enemy" because their government had different interests than ours. Yet, as time takes its course, we begin to study that era in history and realize that the propaganda set out against these people was just that—propaganda.

The government of that country is one thing; however, the people in most cases are similar to us because they have the same human needs. The question is: Why were they judged in such a way? Is this same situation happening now with a different group of people? The way we think and evaluate such issues hopefully has changed and we have become more tolerant and caring of ourselves and others. This last example would be a topic that high school children would be taught to think about. Yet this level of thinking can be used in grade school as well.

The movie *Her Majesty* is a great example of this concept of having different perspectives. The movie tells the true story of a young girl in New Zealand. Her friendship with an old Maori woman shows her that history has two sides—the written history and that of those who were conquered by those who wrote the history. This fact is corroborated by Queen Elizabeth herself. I do not want to give the movie's ending away, but please watch it. My students loved it and saw how two very different perspectives influence history.

I always tell my students that the most powerful tools a person has are his or her own ideas. Thoughts are powerful because they can transform you and others. Once an idea takes hold, it will not stop. It keeps going. My students always ask, "Is that why Martin Luther King's ideas are still with us?" The answer is "Yes." Looking back at history, we see many dictators try to squelch ideas by harming those who thought of them. They might have hurt or even killed those people, but the ideas persevered. Now it is up to us to keep ideas flowing.

I hope this discussion has helped you to understand a bit more about why teachers need your help in conversing with your children. Ideas and thoughts take time to develop. They are little seeds that will develop into full-blown trees when their time is right; we just need to water the ideas by listening and asking questions. We can't do it all on our own because the biggest and most influential teacher of your child is at home—you! We—you and I—can do so much if we work together. Please help me because I want the best for our students and your children.

Thank you for always listening.
Lovingly,
Your child's teacher

LETTER 15

Thinking Levels in the Classroom

Dear Parents,

You have asked me to give you an example of what the thinking process looks like. I thought it might be helpful if I write an example of what it looks like for children in an elementary school. This example should help illustrate the level of thinking abilities your child should have in his or her academic development. (Please remember that everybody develops differently; your child might be ahead or a bit behind, and that is *okay* as long as you see that progress is being made.)

One of my favorite science lessons in first grade is about eggs. Normally, when we start a lesson, teachers have children recall the information they already know on a subject. This recall is quite important because it will be the building block for the new knowledge.

We use different techniques, but for my purpose here, I will describe the KWL chart. This chart is simple. We have three columns on a piece of chart paper. Each column is labeled with a letter. The letter "K" is in the first column and represents "What we already **know**." The middle column is labeled with a "W" and represents

"What we **want** to know or learn." The last column is labeled with an "L" and represents "What we have **learned**."

When we start a lesson, we gather our students and brainstorm any ideas we have on a subject. These ideas will be written down in the "K" column. As we discuss what we know, we will also write down what we want to know about the subject in the "L" column. The final column will be visited periodically. It is my understanding that some lawyers and scientists follow a similar system when they try to piece information together.

Now, please think of the following: When we fill out the column of what we already know, we are tapping into children's experiences and they are using their memories to recall information. The level of thinking is not that high at all. Some of the answers are "I had eggs for breakfast," "I love to eat eggs," and "Chickens lay eggs." You get the picture.

As we move forward into our "What we want to know" column, we begin to tap into the child's understanding. Does the child know that chickens are not the only feathered friends that lay eggs? So a logical question would be, "Children, do other animals lay eggs?" Undoubtedly, the answer will be "Yes." "Ducks and geese do, too." And this is when teachers truly begin to build on the children's knowledge. "How do you know that?" "Turn around and explain to your partner how you know this."

The answers will be many: "My mommy read me a story about a duck," or "My aunt has ducks on her farm." The answers are as diverse as our students are. So what did this simple question do? Well, it had your children recall other information and begin to classify it. When we can classify, we are actually showing understanding. What do the children understand? The children understand that an egg is not only laid by a chicken. Other animals also lay eggs. We can then give them several pictures of different types of eggs (chicken eggs, duck eggs, penguin eggs, etc.).

The children's assignment could be to create categories for the different types of eggs. Are they small or are they large? Are the eggs white or speckled? The children will have to create their own categories based on the observations they are making. To create these categories, they need to communicate what they see and discuss it with their classmates. They will then write down their discoveries or draw them. This task seems simple, but it is not always that easy, especially if you are small.

Once our students have classified the information, the children will be asked to think about it and will be shown other pictures of animals that lay eggs. The thing is that these animals are not cute and feathery; they are cute and slimy (amphibians) or cute and scaly (reptiles). The children will now have to decide what information about the initial study of eggs transfers to these "new eggs."

The children are now transferring information, already learned, to a new setting. Children might be asked to classify the new types of eggs with the old eggs. By doing so, they are going to have to analyze their previous knowledge to determine whether it fits into their original model. As they look at the pictures, they might have to challenge their original ideas and reorganize their pictures into new groups or subgroups.

As adults, it's easy for us to categorize because we have done it many times. Children, however, struggle with categorization. They are not sure of how they should organize the information. It is a discovery process that requires them to play with what they are being asked to categorize. Students need to think of the different types of categories they can create.

As a teacher, it is very interesting to hear the discussion that takes place among students as they decide what they will do. Once they have created their groupings, they need to explain what they did and why they did it. This explanation takes a bit of thought and articulating on their parts—not an easy task. Then comes the harder part—they are asked to decide whether their classifications are correct. If they are, they will need to explain why they are correct. If they are not, they will also have to explain why not.

Many adults even struggle with their own words and how to create an explanation that is simple for their child to understand. Think of a time your child asked you to explain why something is the way it is. Were you patient? Many times, we may answer, "It is like that because that is the way it is." It is hard to explain things correctly all the time. It is harder if we don't have the ability and opportunity to listen to our thinking.

Finally, we are able to have our children move forward in their egg project. We ask them to create new ideas with what they have learned. These ideas might be as simple as "There are many animals that lay eggs" or "Can I make an omelet out of frog eggs?" This last question might seem like a silly one, but it is actually a good one because it will take the kids back to square one. They will create new questions, and they will hopefully follow through the same process they just completed. The difference is that there is new knowledge to be investigated and thought of, and perhaps included.

Thinking is not a stagnant process; it needs to be prodded along the way. As we move along its different levels, we are growing intellectually. The greatest ally we have in this process is observing and questioning what we see and think. Children are inquisitive; that is their nature. When we talk with them, we help them make sense out of their surroundings. You create their surroundings. Discussing what they see and feel lays the foundations for what they will do academically at school.

I hope this example was clear enough. I also hope you feel free to create similar circumstances with your children at home. Have them categorize rocks, different pastas, buttons, or crayons. You have so many choices. When you do remember, you are guiding them, and your actions are telling them you love them.

Lovingly,
Your child's teacher

LETTER 16

How the Thinking Process Develops as Children Grow

Dear Parents,

I will now explain how the thinking process develops as children grow older. Before I do, please let me briefly discuss children who fall within these stages. Understanding this situation will help make things clearer for all of us.

At each stage of learning and development, your children are amazing! They are quirky and are developing their own thought patterns. They truly are thinking, but sometimes their lovely physical development (puberty) makes them seem quite silly. Many of the things we think are common sense are not understandable to them. It is not that they are trying to be ornery or stubborn—they are not. It is just that their hormones are truly getting in the way of clear thinking.

As parents, it is hard at times for us to be patient with our children; patience is not always handy when we need it, and boy do we need it at this stage! Please remember to be patient when your lovely teenager does and says things that, quite frankly, seem plain dumb. She is not necessarily trying to be dumb or to irritate you;

she just hasn't developed clear thinking at this point. Now back to thinking patterns and their development.

In the State of Illinois, the Constitution Test is taken in seventh grade. Knowing the U.S. Constitution is quite important as it shows us our rights and responsibilities, something we should not take lightly. This topic is not something we should read about, take a test on, and then move on from. It is a "live topic," meaning that it is the basis of our democracy, and as such, it needs to be treated as a living document.

We teach our students what the Constitution is and what it represents. Students will read the Constitution and discuss it. Some teachers will use the PBS Liberty Kids program to help bring to life the historical period when the Constitution was created as a way to entertain and educate the students. Yet, all this information is not enough to bring this document to life; we need you, the parents, to help us with this.

Teachers lay the academic foundation for understanding this important document. We present the concepts. We will discuss and analyze the United States' history and what contributed to the formation of this document and our country, what our founding fathers lived through to guarantee us those rights and responsibilities we hold so sacred, and what the actual Constitution means. Yet, all these are abstract thoughts. The children need to begin living them if they are to become responsible citizens of our nation and truly understand what being responsible citizens means, along with knowing the ideals are nation is based upon. It is in living them that these words take on a reality of their own.

You help us bring these concepts to life and help us create true contributing citizens by discussing, analyzing, and helping your children to evaluate many of the political events that happen in our towns, cities, and countries. When you see an event in the news, mention it at the dinner table. Bring up the facts. That is recalling information. Your children might know something about what you are talking about. They might have heard a classmate or teacher mention it. Hopefully, they can contribute more information and ask questions, thereby enriching their knowledge as they converse with you.

The next step is to discuss what these different events mean. As you and your child discuss the meaning of these events, you help your child create new knowledge. This knowledge is important because it will become the foundation for how he or she sees the world. Now, as a teacher, I can teach your children facts and help them think through the information. Doing so will create better understanding and comprehension, but the key is that you are the parent, and what you think and value is what you are going to transfer to your child through these conversations. In a democracy, this matters!

If we want our democracy to continue, it is of great importance that we freely interchange ideas and thoughts with our children about the news, politics, and other such matters. In fact, this process is necessary for our Constitution to continue as a live document.

Now we are ready to move on to our next level of thinking. This level is interesting because in many ways it is a call to action. What do I know? How can I use it to change my environment? When you discuss and then motivate your child into action, you are helping him develop a huge belief in himself. What a gift! So what kind of civic activities can your child engage in? How about knocking on doors to mobilize voters? What about getting a group of friends together to clean a local park or school? No matter how small or big these activities are, you are helping your child develop a sense of "I can contribute. I can give to others. I make a difference in my world."

There is a difference between telling your child he can contribute and actually having him do it. Actually contributing will create a feeling of accomplishment that develops self-esteem. (Many of us confuse self-esteem with being told we are loved and believed in. Yet, it is "in the doing" where we truly see a difference in our child's self-esteem). Ralph Waldo Emerson illustrates this best when he says, "Thought is the blossom; language the bud; action the fruit behind it. The ancestor of every action is a thought and skill comes of doing."

When we are "doing," we are able to notice patterns and reorganize our ideas. Maybe what we thought would be easy, isn't so. Maybe what we perceived as somebody's carelessness, in our first discussion, is not carelessness. Maybe these people were doing their best and things were a bit more complicated. Your child needs to understand the complications of doing.

In our initial discussions, we might not see what is truly behind some opinions or actions. However, when we start doing, we might realize that things are different and much more complex. Being able to recognize the complexity added with multiple viewpoints and perspectives usually comes from experience and putting ourselves in somebody else's shoes. Students need to have this skill if they are to become true problem solvers. When we only see one side of the equation, we will have a harder time problem solving.

Recognizing multiple viewpoints takes us to our next step: analyzing. When things work out or don't, it is necessary to stop and figure out what went well and what didn't. This analysis is truly important because it gives us insight into what we need to do to improve. Recognizing our strengths allows us to continue building on them. Recognizing our weaknesses helps us improve, too.

When we are able to sit down and discuss with our child what we think went right with him and his friends passing out flyers to get people to vote, we are empowering him. Our conversation should sound something like this:

"Honey, I see you still have many of the flyers."

"Yes, most people did not want them because they think that their votes do not make a difference."

"Wow! What do you think?"

"I don't know."

"So, do you agree with them?"

"Maybe, but…"

"So, you are not sure."

"Well, if all of us voted…"

"Would that make a difference?"

"Yes, I guess so."

"How's that?"

"Well, all of our votes are important, and when we don't vote, we are the ones who are deciding that it does not make a difference."

"I'm impressed—those are powerful words. So what are you going to do now?"

"I'm not sure, but maybe…."

You get the point; the possibilities are endless. It is in these types of dialogues that our students experience their greatest growth. Did you notice there was no lecturing on the adult's side? There doesn't need to be. Remember, this process is about children discovering their own potential. It is a discovery lesson, and the true potential for growth is in discovering our own answers.

And we then move up to the next step in our ladder of thought: synthesizing. Here our children bring in old information and break it down in order to create new thoughts and ideas. Please pay close attention to the following dialogue:

"You know, Mom, I was thinking about the voting."

"Oh?"

"Well, I think voting is important because it can make things change."

"I see."

"Well, at school, we were learning that the one time we are all truly equal is when we vote."

"Oh."

"But when we don't vote, we are giving away our right and responsibility. We are letting others decide for us. I think that is not OKAY."

"I see you have been thinking about this."

"So, if people are not motivated, we need to do something."

"Well, what do you think can be done?"

"I'm not sure that passing out flyers was successful. Most people were not even home."

"It must have been frustrating."

"Mom, it was!"

"So what can you do then?"

"Well, I was thinking that my friends and I could ask our teachers if we could talk to each class for five minutes."

"Oh, what would you talk about?"

"Well, the importance of getting their parents to vote."

"Oh! It sounds feasible."

"Well, they can ask their parents to take them to the voting booth so they can see what it is like. That way, they are asking their parents to teach them, and at the same time, getting them to vote."

"Pretty tricky!"

"Yeah! I know. Do you think it will work?"

"Give it a try and let's see what happens."

We are finally at the last step in our thinking ladder: evaluating. When we evaluate, we assess and make judgments. Did it work? Was my first idea a good one, or was changing tactics better? Why? Answering our own questions brings the whole cycle of thinking around. We come back to where we initially started with a new understanding and a greater depth of knowledge.

The point is that the knowledge we have acquired was never truly about the initial discussion we had about the news article; it was about how we discovered our strengths and weaknesses through our actions. That is the magic of teaching!

Gaining this type of knowledge is not an easy task; it takes years of development. Please believe me that when we start out, it is daunting. Yet most teachers face this task alone. We need your ideas and conversations to help us create a better society—a society in which all of us can express our thoughts. The way we can begin to create that better society is by creating a dialogue over time with your children about what life, liberty, and the pursuit of happiness mean to you.

Now, please do not rush to have a lengthy conversation with your child. These thoughts are developed gradually. They are developed through constant dialogues about common day occurrences, what we see in the news, and other things. There is always something in life worth commenting on.

So my homework for you is please to keep talking to your children. We—you and I—make a difference.

As always, I hope this information makes things a bit more clear.

Thank you for listening,
Lovingly,
Your child's teacher

LETTER 17

Measuring Thinking Levels with Tests

Dear Parents,

In the last example, I shared how the thinking process develops. As you can see, teachers and parents help students develop some pretty high level thinking skills. One method many teachers use to help further their students' thinking is asking questions. This is called the Socratic Method.

I want to give you an example of these types of questions and what we teachers are looking for in terms of responses when we ask them. I think this discussion will make understanding the thinking process clearer for you, and it will then lead us into the subject of grades.

To do so, I will tell you a little story and give you some multiple choice answers. Then we will discuss the answers and choose the best one. My example will relate to children in first and second grades. Here is the story:

Grandma had some very yummy strawberries and thought that her granddaughter, Danita, would like some. So, she gave Danita a small plate with strawberries. Danita was about to eat them when she saw that her little brother wanted some strawberries, too. She then gave her little brother, Johnny, the strawberries to eat.

Johnny took the strawberries. He was about to eat them when he saw his father working very hard in the garage. Johnny thought that his father would enjoy eating the strawberries because he was working so hard and they were juicy. His father thanked him and went into the kitchen to wash his hands and eat the strawberries when he saw his wife. Boy, did she like strawberries! So he gave her the strawberries, and as he was about to go back outside, the rest of the family came in. When they saw the strawberries, they all began to laugh and decided to share the strawberries.

This is a very simple story, but if we are lucky, we are able to relate to it. Now, if we have the children read the above story and answer the following question, I can guarantee that more than three-fourths of my class will get the answer wrong. So let's look at the question.

What is this story about?

a. A family who eats strawberries

b. A family who likes to share

c. A family who gets along

d. A family who loves each other

Let's consider answer A. By reading the story, one can tell that the family loves to eat strawberries. But the story is not about eating strawberries. It does not tell us whether they eat the strawberries with ice cream or anything else. So, the answer is not the letter A.

Now, let's consider answer B. Yes, it does seem like the family likes to share, but is the story really about sharing? Does it give other examples of them sharing toys or candy? It doesn't. Therefore, the answer is not the letter B.

The next answer is C, which suggests the story is about a family who gets along. We do see that the family gets along well. After all, they are all sharing strawberries together, but they are not giving us more examples of them getting along. After sharing the strawberries, they could have an argument or become upset with each other. But these answers are simple answers; in many ways, they are evident since they only deal with recalling and understanding information.

Answer D asks us to go a bit further with our thinking skills, we realize that we need to interpret what type of relationship this family has. It is a caring one. They are willing to forfeit something they truly enjoy because they love each other. So yes, they love strawberries and will share them with each other because they are a loving family. So the higher thinking answer is D: A family who loves each other.

As adults, we are able to see and understand why D is the correct answer. Yet, younger children will choose answers A or B because they are obvious and concrete. The story speaks about strawberries and sharing. It does not speak of a loving family in a concrete way. That love, however, was always implied. Being able to abstract this knowledge is an ability that comes from discussing events and relationships we see within our daily circumstances. When we speak of these concepts with our children, we help them begin to think abstractly. The higher level thinking skills are abstract.

Teachers teach children how to develop higher level thinking skills. We give our children ample opportunities to practice and develop them. However, as with all skills, your input and contribution is needed. Your daily, everyday interactions help children develop these thinking patterns.

When you analyze daily events with your children, you help form your child's own conclusions and help him or her move up into more abstract thinking. Once you and your child have come to a conclusion, have him explain why he thinks that. The more often you go through this process with your child, the better he will be able to express his thoughts. Remember, it will be in an oral way at first, and later on, in a written way.

As I always say, you are such an integral part of your child's education. So, let's keep talking!

Lovingly,
Your child's teacher

LETTER 18

Developing Your Child's Thinking Skills

Dear Parents,

In my previous letter, I said I wanted to explain grades to you. However, you asked me to give you some ideas about how you can help your child develop good thinking skills. So that is what I will do first.

But before I begin, I want to make sure you understand that this process will take time. It starts at infancy and early childhood and develops as your child grows. You can help the process along, but you will also have to let it develop at its own pace.

You can water and fertilize a child's mind. But then you have to wait and let it grow. All this has to be done with lots of love and patience. I really mean patience (lots and lots of it). If you feel you are running low on it, try to remember a special moment with your child. Doing so always helps me stay motivated, especially after a long frustrating hour or two of explaining something and not seeing the lightbulb turn on in the child's mind. However, if you tend your garden properly, the rewards are always amazing.

The other thing you need to know is that if you can help along this process in a fun but very firm way, you have helped yourself immensely. It will have taken a lot of the sting out of thinking and trying to do homework for both you and your child.

So, here we go. This is Thinking 101.

As you know, most thinking by children is expressed orally, so the ideas we will focus on will be easy to implement because you can practice them anywhere. You can develop your child's skills as you are walking down the street, riding in the car, shopping at the grocery store, eating at the dinner table, or even while you are watching TV. If you choose to develop your child's skills while you are watching TV, commercial time is best.

The key is conversing with your child. There is no one way to do it. You know your child best. The thing you want to do is take real life events and discuss them. An example could be: "So you also noticed Aunt Sarah was in a bad mood? What do you think it was all about? She seemed rather upset, but I did not dare ask why." Let your children answer these questions. The process helps them develop as they try to make sense of their world. When they answer, you should listen and paraphrase what is being said. Keep the conversation going as you would with a friend.

Let's now analyze your child's response. "Well, I think Aunt Sarah was mad at Johnny." In this simple sentence, your child just recalled information, interpreted it, and summarized it. It does not matter whether he is wrong or right; you can always correct him later. What matters is that he was able to take information and piece it together to make sense of his world. He was also able to express it.

In the next part, "Johnny did not do his homework so the teacher called Aunt Sarah for a meeting with the principal. This is the third time this month." Here he is actually analyzing the different things he knows and putting them together into a coherent idea. Now sometimes you may think Johnny must have told your child this information. But the fact remains that Johnny could have told your child only bits and pieces of the whole scenario, in which case, your child is interpreting it and coming up with his own conclusions.

"You know, Mom, I think Aunt Sarah is mad at Johnny, but I really think that she is worried about him. She is annoyed at having to go to a meeting and mad at herself because she doesn't know what to do about Johnny." This sentence is very powerful. Your child was just able to understand, analyze, and evaluate a difficult situation using higher thinking skills. Most kids are capable of this type of thinking if we give them the opportunity.

Now I am aware that many people say you don't discuss older family members with your children. And you are right; in most cases, you shouldn't. But sometimes you need to. It helps clarify family relationships. Your child is not blind or deaf; he or she can perceive things just fine. Pretending things don't happen is like having an elephant in the room and nobody talking about it. You don't need to give explanations; just ask your child what he perceived and why he perceived it that way. You will be amazed by how perceptive your child is.

One last thing: Do not shut your child's theories down, even if they are wrong. Guiding the conversation to the right answer is so much more effective because through your guiding, you will enhance your child's thinking capacities. You will show him that there are different ways of getting to a conclusion and that not everything is the way we see it. If you ask me, you just taught your child a true life lesson.

The importance of this lesson is not only academic. This lesson is truly a life lesson. When you listen to your child, truly listen, you are telling him that what he says has value. You are telling him that you think his ideas are important and can contribute to understanding others. You are letting him know that he can perceive and discuss without hurting others. Most importantly, you just showed your child, through your actions, that he is valued by you. Now that is a great way to build self-esteem!

Now the academic component: If your child is able to perceive these events and interpret them adequately, that skill will be transferred to his reading and writing. He will be able to read an article, listen to a conference, be involved in a conversation, and so on, and decide for himself if what he is being told is right for him or not. This ability will in turn show up in his essays.

Now when your child is asked to write an essay on his position of the use of green energy vs. petroleum, he will be able to look at two different perspectives and evaluate them, feeling confident that he is capable of interpreting things correctly from his own point of view. It does not matter to him if others agree with him or not. This is self-confidence!

See what can be accomplished with patience, love, good listening skills, and an open heart and ears. A lot more than you thought, right?

Thank you for opening your heart and mind to me and especially your children.

Lovingly,
Your child's teacher

LETTER 19

Helping Your Child Explore His or Her Own Ideas

Dear Parents,

You said you like how I tied in a simple conversation to thinking skills. You said it showed you how the different levels of thinking skills were present within a conversation. You said it was the first time you thought of conversations with your child in a different light. I am so pleased.

You also said that you are not completely sure how this topic ties into your child's academic writing, and therefore, you needed me to tie it in for you to understand a bit better. Let me try to explain it, and then I will move on to how you can continue to use the little but important moments in your daily life to help your kids improve at school.

The conversation I gave as an example, in my previous letter, is actually a true example. It ties into your child's writing by helping your child express ideas that are being created in his head. When you are listening to what is being said, you are allowing your child to put his ideas in order. You are allowing him to clarify what he is thinking.

Many times we have ideas, but we are not sure how to express them. They are all jumbled up. We need to express them to help us understand them. When we ask small questions, simple ones, we are actually furthering the thinking process a bit. We are not telling our kids the actual answers. Simply telling your child the answers will not allow him or her to grow intellectually—a mistake that so many of us make inadvertently. We normally just tell our children to go do something else or give them the answer. For example, saying, "Aunt Sarah is having problems with Johnny" rather than asking our child why he thinks Aunt Sarah seems upset and letting him reason out the situation, as I explained in my last letter.

As you can see, sending our child away or giving him the correct answer keeps him from figuring things out for himself. Our kids are smart—they really are! We sometimes find ourselves buried under so many responsibilities that we forget what is most important—conversing with our children. When we fail to remember what is important, we forfeit our right and responsibility to get to know our children fully.

It is through these conversations that we are able to see who our children are, what they truly like, and what makes them tick. In the movie *A Better Life*, the father works extremely hard to give his son a better life. It is evident that he cares deeply about his son. He will do anything to improve his son's life, yet his circumstances do not allow him to do the one thing that matters most—spend quality time with his son. When life forces the father and son to spend time together, the son is truly able to see his father's integrity of character. For the first time, he is able to recognize his father's worth as a person and not just as a provider. It is through the small conversations they have that the son is able to understand the higher meaning of things. And these higher meanings are the meat and juice of most academic work.

When I ask your child to write, most children say, "I don't know what to write" or "I don't have anything to say." Why do students think this? Well, because, most of our students have not had the opportunity to be truly heard. They don't realize that their everyday life occurrences are important. They don't realize that these everyday life occurrences form their thinking and their perceptions. They don't realize that we write what we know.

Many of our students don't realize they know things that are important to them and others. Why? Because, they have not been given the opportunity to explore and express their ideas with a patient listener, who is there for them.

At school, we do something called "think, pair share." Children are given an idea to explore and think about. Yet, the idea needs to be expressed and challenged or confirmed. The children then turn to their partners and express their thinking. They get a chance to say what they think and why. It is quite powerful.

When kids start doing "pair share," they normally look at each other, not knowing what to say. They are not sure of themselves and their answers. "What if somebody thinks I am dumb?" "What if my answer is wrong?" What if…and so it goes in a downward spiral. Yet, there are many reasons why a child is not comfortable expressing his ideas or beliefs. Such expression can be hard even for some adults. But as all teachers know, if we continue through the process, children begin to realize that even if their ideas are not correct, they can lead them to some interesting discoveries. Hearing their ideas out loud makes them tangible in a way. The ideas may still be abstract, but somehow, they now are more real and valid. Having them confirmed or challenged helps the learning process.

Consider this: At school, we have little time to pair share and interchange ideas because we have so much curriculum to cover. Many times, we can't cover some subjects to the depth we would like. However, this does not have to be an issue if you start pair sharing with your children. The process is simple, very simple. Ask them about something they learned at school. Ask them to explain it to you. Ask them questions that you might have about the subject. (Have them write down the questions so they can discuss them and find the answers when they come to class.) Ask them what they think about what they learned. If they say the topic was boring, ask them why it was boring. Ask them whether it might be useful to them even if it is boring. All these questions are designed to help children develop their thinking.

Many of us have gotten away from these types of questions because we find we have other distractions. Yet, we need to get back to conversing with our children. These conversations help them and us by developing their thinking and giving us a deeper knowledge of our children. It is a "win-win" situation for us all.

Thank you for your interest.
Lovingly,
Your child's teacher

LETTER 20

Engaging in Fun Activities That Help Learning

Dear Parents,

After my previous letters, you said you wanted your interactions with your child to be more educational and playful. You also mentioned that you want to help your child develop his thinking a bit more. The problem, you said, is that many of the school activities you do with your child require paper and pencil. These activities feel tedious to you and your child; therefore, you prefer something that does not become a constant challenge where you have to argue with your child to get him or her to do her homework. Instead of a battle with your child, you want an activity that fosters a greater dialogue between the two of you.

In response to your request, I have thought of some activities that are fun and educational at the same time. They will help develop academic skills, but most importantly, they will turn into a sharing time with your child. The fun part is that they can be played anywhere. Remember, it is a game, so you need to keep it fun. So, here we go….

Let's say you are in the car. As you are driving along, give your child some words that have opposites, and ask your child to give you its opposite word. For example: Black-white, short-tall, fat-thin, big-little, up-down. You get the point. It is a very easy game, and little ones get a kick out of it. Now, let me tell you how this simple game helps your child academically. It develops your child's vocabulary and quickness of thought. Why is this important? Well, expressing ourselves requires vocabulary.

A rich vocabulary helps us express a plethora of feelings and thoughts. Think about it; saying, "I am happy" is not the same as saying, "I am ecstatic." Both words express a form of happiness, but one is a calmer, more at peace kind of happiness, while the other is an exploding sense of happiness. Increasing your child's vocabulary allows him to have the language to express higher levels of thinking. The quick tempo of the game helps with the recall of facts.

We want our children to be quick and witty with their thinking. Sometimes, a quick answer is needed, and you want your child to be able to think on his feet. Practice helps with this skill.

Another game you can play easily with your child is sounding out syllables in a word. Do you remember playing this game at school? The teacher would say a word and you would separate it by syllables. Remember? Flower was flow-er. Running was run-ning. Apple was ap-ple. Tapping out the syllables of these words was enjoyable. This simple game can be played anywhere and will be of great benefit to your child.

Practicing this simple skill helps your child hear the different sounds in a word so he or she can figure out how to write and spell it. Do you want to take this exercise a step further? Have your child clap out each sound or separate letters and sounds in a word. The word ball would be b-a-ll. The word song would be s-o-n-g. To make these exercises fun, you can say the first sound and he can say the next sound. You can take turns.

Last summer, I played this game with a little boy. At first, the clapping was okay, but somehow, the game changed into a ball game. We passed the ball to each other. Whoever had the ball had to say the next sound or letter in the word we were spelling. Both the boy and I enjoyed the game and so can you. Be creative; I bet both of you can come up with a different game using the same principle. Practice is what matters here. Try it.

As you are cooking, you can practice spelling by having your child sound out words and then have him move a bean or counter to match each sound. Let's say he is spelling the word "ball." He will say the "b" sound and move a counter. Next, he will say the "a" sound and move another counter. Finally, he will say the "l" sound and move another counter. He will then look at his three counters and say b-a-ll in rapid succession. Once he gets good at spelling the words, you can have him write the letters that match the sounds he hears. This simple skill helps him focus on what he is hearing. It also helps him improve his spelling, and therefore, his writing.

Many children will begin to write using inventive spelling (a word is spelled out according to how it sounds to them). If we want to help them improve their spelling skills, this game is a good way to do it. Your children will enjoy the game as they learn how to spell, but the true benefit of this game is the bonding time they share with you.

We all learn and retain information best when we have something pleasant to associate it with. In a child's life, nothing can top spending a wonderful time with Mom or Dad. These moments are the ones that will become your child's cherished memories of sharing time with you.

Lovingly,
Your child's teacher

LETTER 21

Learning Activities That Foster Thinking

Dear Parents,

You liked the previous ideas. Good! But now, you want more. That is a good thing. Let me tell you about one of my favorite learning techniques. I love this one because it is so simple, and it truly fosters communication and thinking.

As you watch TV, it does not matter what show, do the following: Ask questions about the show and listen to what your children are saying. It is through their answers that you will be able to figure out what to ask next. Now, this activity is truly important because you will be guiding their academic and moral growth as well. Here is where you truly see what your children value. So, how do you begin? Let me explain with an example.

Let's say you are watching the movie *Soul Surfer*. This movie is the true story of a teenage girl who loses her arm to a shark while surfing. Somehow through inner courage, she finds the strength to continue until she becomes a world champion surfer. As you are watching the movie with your kids, pause the film because you or your spouse have to go to the bathroom, get more popcorn, etc.

As the rest of you wait, start asking questions: "What do you think is going to happen?" "Why do you think that?" "What do you think the character is feeling?" "Would you feel the same way?" "Why?" When you are ready, restart the movie and see whether your children's predictions were correct. Discuss them. Yes, I know it is horrible to watch a movie with interruptions and somebody asking questions, but find a way to be cool about it because you want to keep your kids engaged.

Asking these questions might be frustrating and a bit annoying for your child, but try not to let your kids off the hook when they say it was just "good" or anything of that sort. Remember, you are striving for longer and well-thought out answers; keep in mind that your goal is to create higher level thinkers.

This discussion helps your children because since they are watching a movie, it is tangible rather than too abstract. They don't have to draw an image in their heads. They can see and hear it. From the concrete, you can move to the abstract by using questioning. As an example, the following dialogue should help make things clear. Here, I'll imagine addressing teenagers because they can be a bit more difficult. However, if you start this process with younger children, it should be much simpler to do.

"Hey, what do you think about this movie I brought home from the video store? It looks like a good one."

"Yeah."

"What do you think it is about?"

"I don't know. Read the back of the box."

"Well, the summary says it is about this girl who experiences a life-changing event. It sounds interesting."

"If you say so." (I know this kind of response can be a bit unnerving and annoying, to say the least, but stick with it.)

Once you've started watching, the movie, continue the conversation:

"Hey, I told you it was pretty good. It seems you like it."

"Mom!"

"OKAY, I will be quiet."

(At a good point in the movie, pause it. Most movies have built in parts where you can stop the movie right before something interesting happens. These points are the ones you take advantage of.)

"Hey, while Dad gets more popcorn, tell me what you think is going to happen."

"Most likely they are going to save her."

"Yes, but how?"

"Well, I don't know."

"I think they are going to have to call someone."

"Mom, they can't; they're in the middle of the water."

"Oh, that's right. So what do you think they are going to do?"

"Well, maybe they have to take her to the shore and…."

Later, as the movie continues, whisper, "Hey, your prediction was almost right."

"Yeah, I know."

I hope this example gives you a good idea of what you can do. There are an unlimited number of questions you can ask. The point is that you get your children thinking and expressing.

When you ask what the movie is about, you are making your child look at the cover of the movie and interpret it. Normally, the images and title will give us the main idea about a movie or book. Your child will have to take those clues and find a way of expressing what they are telling her.

All readers and writers need to be able to identify the main idea, even if it is while watching a movie. Remember my example in Letter 17 about the family who shared their strawberries? The main idea was that each family member loved the others enough to forfeit the pleasure of eating the strawberries and to pass them on to another family member who would enjoy them more. Yet, if this story were to be made into a real book, maybe the book's cover would show a picture of the family eating strawberries. Would we be able to tell the book is about family members giving up their strawberries so another family member can enjoy them? Not really.

This is the beauty of predicting. You get surprises here and there because you are going to build your prediction on what you already know and what is familiar to you. So when you ask the question, you are asking your daughter to recall what she knows—to interpret it and incorporate it into the new information she is receiving.

When you ask her to tell you how she thinks the problem is going to be solved, she will once again have to interpret the whole situation and piece it together. In many ways, she is synthesizing and analyzing the information to create something new. It does not matter that the new creation is a thought. This thought will contribute to other thoughts that will continue to grow and develop.

If we focus on the prediction part, in which you say, "Hey, your prediction was almost right," then you are actually giving your child credit for something well thought-out. Kids like to be acknowledged. We all do! This acknowledgment will carry you a long way because it is substantial. In other words, your child has taken a type of action that makes your praise real. Think about it. You can tell when "Good job" is said to you in earnest or not. Many times, we praise behavior for things that are trivial, without much validity. Kids can see how hollow this type of praise is. Look for situations with depth when you offer praise.

As always, I hope this information helps make things a bit clearer for you.

Lovingly,
Your child's teacher

LETTER 22

Connecting Ideas and Writing

Dear Parents,

You want me to explain how to apply the previous questioning technique (the one we used with the movie in the last letter) to reading and writing. As always, I promise to do my best. Reading and writing both work in a similar way. They make concrete thoughts into abstract ones and vice versa. This is their nature. So when we talk about asking questions, we are trying to get our kids to think and express their thoughts.

The technique is easy. Begin it as a conversation between you and your child. As long as it feels like a dialogue, you will be successful. The second it turns into an interrogation, the doors will be shut. The other thing to keep in mind throughout the conversation is not to preach. It does not matter whether or not you have the answer. Nobody likes to be preached to, which can sound like a lecture and, often times, a scolding. Remember, the mission is not to give knowledge; it is to help your children gain it through self-discovery. (Even if that sometimes means playing dumb.)

When your child is reading (strive for a minimum goal of thirty minutes per day), discuss the story he or she is reading. You don't need to discuss it while the reading is being done; you can do it afterwards, maybe while eating dinner or before bedtime.

A good way to begin is to ask what is going on in the book your child is reading. Ask her to explain it to you. As she begins to explain, pay close attention to what is being described and formulate the following types of questions and confirmations: "Wow, so what do you think is going to happen?" (predicting), "Oh, why do you think she is going to do that?" (interpreting the character's motives), "Really? You hadn't told me that." (showing interest in what your child has to say), and "You are going to have to tell me what happens next. I'm hooked." (confirming your child is right in predicting).

All these questions are the ones you would ask when somebody describes a TV show or movie. We all ask these types of questions when we are talking with a friend. Why not engage our children in these types of conversations about their reading? Sometimes, we think we don't have anything to say to our kids because we normally don't dialogue with them, so this kind of conversation can be a starting point.

If your child does not like to read, watch what he is watching on TV and try asking questions just like you would with a friend at work when you discuss the latest show. Granted, you might not have the same interests as your child, but try to see things from his or her point of view. I have read several book collections with this intention. My kids and I both loved the Percy Jackson series by Rick Riordan. It got to the point where they would not tell me what was going to happen so I would have to read the books.

I have also discovered that as we analyze the plots and complexities of stories, kids show that they have quite a few ideas of their own. The interesting thing is that they can relate themes and common ideas to other books, people, and circumstances. Teachers call this relationship "world-to-self connections" and "text-to-self connections." These connections are great because they mean that our children are remembering similar circumstances and interpreting them. They continue to break down the information and compare and contrast it with what they are reading (or seeing, if they are watching a show). They then evaluate it and decide whether it is similar or different. That is a lot of thinking!

Now what do you have to do? Say things like, "Wow! I had not thought about that. Explain it to me." That's all. Your child will be thrilled because you are paying attention. Your listening shows him that he is valued by you. (Doesn't this beat buying a toy or gadget to make your child feel valued?) Now your actions are helping your child's self-esteem grow. Your child knows that what he says is worthwhile. His self-esteem isn't based on false praise like, "I think you are cool." No, it is based in the people who matter the most—Mom and Dad—thinking he has interesting things to say.

What a gift you have given your child! Imagine the power of this small incident multiplied a thousand times. You and I can make this difference! We are capable of helping your child. Let's work together at this simple task because once it gets going…well, we never know what it might lead to…but one thing is certain—it will lead to great relationships and good writing.

You wanted to know how building your child's self-esteem connects to his writing. Well, he understands he has a voice, a wonderful voice, that says he is interesting and has worthwhile things to say. Now we are ready to begin the writing process.

I know I speak for all teachers when I say this: Thank you! You make a difference in the classroom!

Lovingly,
Your child's teacher

LETTER 23

Setting Boundaries Is Important

Dear Parents,

I hope the previous ideas have been helpful to you. Please remember that each one of us is different and so are our children. The key to working with these ideas is that you do it at your own pace, and more importantly, that you find a way to balance them out. When considering them and their impact on your child's thinking and writing, you are the one who knows your child best. The only one who can set the correct pace for your family is you.

Some moments are easier than others for following through and conversing with your child. Sometimes, you do not want to talk. You are tired or cranky, or you just want to be in your own little bubble and truly do not feel like listening to your child. You know it is okay to be human; we have to respect when we feel that way because if we don't, we become an empty jar without much to give.

I have learned to honor those times. I need "Me Time" and so do *you*. Please know that this game, called parenting, is a huge juggling game, and the person who needs to be taken care of first is you. So if you say, "No," honor your right to say, "No." That does not make you or me a bad parent. It just makes us human. Let your child know that. So many parents don't know how to honor themselves. It is necessary for them to do so. When they do honor themselves, their children will begin to honor them as well.

Many years ago, my whole family was watching TV. All of us were hungry and my dad got up to make us a snack. As the treats took longer and longer to come, I got up to see why they were taking so long. Well, they were not coming because my dad was sitting down eating his. I remember asking him why he hadn't gotten snacks for all of us. His answer was a simple one. "I need to make sure I take care of myself before I can properly take care of you." He understood that meeting his immediate hunger was important for him if he wanted to help his family meet theirs.

A few nights ago, I was in bed trying to fall asleep when my daughter came in to talk. Granted, I love talking with her, but I was trying to fall asleep, and it wasn't a critical life or death situation. I told her I would talk to her in the morning and I did. We were able to talk in the car as I drove her to her friend's house.

My point is: Take care of yourself, too. Do what you can and try to find a balance that works for you. The book *Boundaries* by Dr. Henry Cloud and Dr. John Townsend provides great insight into how you can do so, even with your family. The book shows you how to provide strong but gentle parameters to those you love. If you are like many of us who have a hard time saying "No" to others, this book might help. It helped me, and I know it can help you.

Before I continued with discussing writing, I just wanted to remind you that you matter and you are important. The changes you are achieving with your child can sometimes be difficult and even, at times, make you feel alone. Know you are not alone. There are many resources to help you along the way. Reach out for them. You are an amazing parent just because you care enough to change in order to help your child. That in itself speaks volumes.

Hang in there and know that the rewards are well worth it.
Lovingly,
Your child's teacher

LETTER 24

Developing Language Skills

Dear Parents,

As I was preparing to discuss writing with you, I realized we have not spoken about the little ones. This awareness came as I heard a mother speak to her toddler at the grocery store.

As I walked through the store, selecting my groceries, I watched and began to think about infants and toddlers' development. Little ones acquire language at an incredible speed. According to what I have studied, children pick up language through constant interactions with those around them. They observe our body language and listen to the sounds we make. They pay attention to our tone of voice, and they are able to interpret quite accurately what is happening. This ability is extremely important in their development because it sets up all the building blocks our children will need at school and in life in general. The more we interact with them, the better it is for their development.

I was thinking about how children learn when I saw another mother with her child. This mother was tired and needed a break. She pulled out her cell phone and gave it to her child. He became distracted with the phone and allowed her to continue her shopping. This toddler was receiving some sort of stimulation, but there was no body language to help him interpret what he saw. In many ways, he was a "passive learner." Even though he was pressing buttons, he was not getting the full benefit of interacting with another person. (Please know that I am not criticizing. I have found myself in that position many times, and I understand that we all need a break.)

Watching this second mother, I recalled a conversation with a friend who is a speech therapist. She has told me that in recent years, she has seen many children who have not developed language skills, such as talking properly, expressing themselves, language processing (the process of how we understand the concepts that we hear), and other language development problems. What she finds sad is that many of these cases are avoidable if parents will only interact and talk more with their children. Just keep that in mind.

She gave me an easy exercise that might help mothers and fathers develop their toddlers' language and thinking skills. You might be very familiar with it as something you remember from your own childhood.

Go to the grocery store, farmers market, or any type of store, and point out to your child the different vegetables, fruits, meats, or dairy products you see. Name them and pick them up so your child can hold them. Some of you might fear that your child will squish the products. Yes, he or she might, but the point is that you are going to show your child how to hold them. It is better to teach them, at first, how to hold and interact with things and people, than to live with a little "destroyer."

Most kids want to please you. If you take the time to show them how to do things and let them practice, they will be able to do them. Think about it. "Honey, this is a peach; it is very, very delicate. Let me show you how to hold it. Put your two hands around it, like this. Do you want to try holding it?" "Yes!" "Okay. Try to be a bit gentler. Yes that is better." "Oh!" "I see it fell and the peach bruised. Let's put it in a bag and pay for it. We will try again next time. It was a good first try."

This process seems time-consuming, and it is, but the benefits of doing it are huge because you are actually teaching the child. He will learn, and he will transfer this knowledge to other settings. An example of how this lesson will benefit your child is when you go to your friend's house and she does not have to put everything away because she knows your child behaves.

Let's go back to the grocery store. As your child holds the vegetables, discuss them with him. Is the turnip smooth or rough? What does the cabbage smell like? As you put it in a bag, decide if it is heavy or light. Weigh it and then talk about it. You might go as far as deciding to prepare something with him. "Hey, when we get back, we can wash the cucumber and try it with lemon and salt."

By having these simple conversations, you will help create a large and varied vocabulary for your child to express him- or herself. You help build background knowledge for him to draw from when he is at school. Most importantly, you will create those bonding moments with your child. Those last a lifetime.

Lovingly,
Your child's teacher

LETTER 25

Developing Stories and Creativity

Dear Parents,

I just remembered another very simple and easy game you can play with your children. It also can be played anywhere and at any time. The only thing you need is a story and a kid. Isn't that easy?

First, we will start with a made up or true story. As we get better at telling stories, we will transfer them onto paper, either as a drawing or in written form. I guess at the end you will need a pencil and some paper. So, here we go.

While you are in the car, having dinner or running errands, start telling your child a story. Feel free to make it up if you need to. These are always the best stories because your kids can be the main characters. Let me start with a story. This is one my parents used for my siblings and me:

"One Saturday morning, there were these children who lived at _____."

"That is our house!"

"Oh!"

"So what are the kids' names?"

"Jorge, Johnny, Lydia, and Dana."

"Oh! That is us!"

"Yes, it is. Anyway they went to the zoo to see a giraffe."

"Like we did!"

"I guess we did. While their mommy and daddy took them to the zoo, they saw a purple tongue."

"It belonged to the giraffe!"

As you can see, the children are actually helping to recall or create the story. This is good because they are using their imaginations and ability to recall information. When they imagine and recall events, they begin to piece ideas and information together. They might decide that the giraffe's purple tongue is due to eating purple ice cream. That is a totally valid idea. What you are striving for is storytelling of any sort. It gets kids thinking and imagining.

This silly example brings a small moment to life. Your children can add to it as you continue the story. The point is that some of the best stories are those that express a very small period of time. We do not have to talk about what happened in the morning, at the zoo, and finally, on the way back home. If we help our children focus on a small concrete idea, we will help them bring details into that small scenario.

Let me give you a small example of what a kid's initial writing might be and then what we as teachers are trying to achieve.

"Today we got up and went to the park. We went and played and then went to the slide and the swings and the sandpit. Then we went home."

This small example is very similar to what we can expect from a first grader. Yet, we as teachers need children to focus on small incidents because that is where we find depth and richness of language and thought. The previous example is a listing of things or events that happened at the park. Let me now show you an example of what good writing for a writer beginning second grade looks like:

When I was playing at the park, my friend, Josh, found a bucket. We took it to the sandpit and played for a long time. First, we pretended it was a dragon that ate all the sand. It was very, very hungry! Then, we wanted to make a castle, and we filled up the bucket with sand and turned it upside down. The castle was big. We used a stick to make a flag. Finally, we had to say goodbye to our sandcastle and left the bucket.

See the difference? This second narrative is small and full of details. We can picture the kids playing in the sand. Compared to the other writing, it is focused; it has a beginning, a middle, and an end. It also uses sequencing words like "first," "then," and "next" correctly. This type of writing is achievable. Your child can write like this if we help him focus and think about the process—from beginning to end.

There are many ways to teach writing, but a very powerful one is to have students recall important moments in their lives. When they recall these moments, they become inspired. At first, they might say something very simple, such as, "I went to the park." Then we work to develop this idea. Through talking with them we guide their thinking. For example:

"Why did you go to the park?"

"Mom and Dad took me."

"Oh, you went with your mom and dad. I see your sister went, too."

"Yes."

"What did you do at the park?"

"We looked for squirrels."

"It must have been fun!"

"It was. The squirrels were running all over the trees."

You get the point; we are helping the child to express what he or she is living. It is much easier when our students are used to conversing with others. Then it is not such a foreign concept to them.

This task is not easy. The majority of students struggle with knowing what to write. They don't realize the importance of those small interactions in their lives. They do not realize that all of the details that make an event relevant are central to a good piece of writing.

As children recall these important moments in their lives, they begin to define themselves as individuals. The discovery of what matters to them through their conversations and writing allows them to analyze what they value. The more they interact with you, the more their values will reflect yours. You are the one who molds and shapes your child. What you do and say has a huge effect on his life.

Teachers help mold your child academically, but the true molding is done by you, just as it should be. Then it shows up at school.

Lovingly,
Your child's teacher

P.S. I learned about having children write about small moments in their lives through Lucy Calkins. Her writing program taught me a lot. Look her up under The Lucy Calkins Project. Check it out!

LETTER 26

Developing Your Child's Brain

Dear Parents,

When my daughter was very young, I went to see Dr. Bruce Perry speak at a college. Dr. Perry has taught at the very prestigious University of Chicago and is presently at Northwestern University, and he does research on how to help children who experience crises in their lives. He is world-renowned, and more importantly, his research can teach us a lot about how interacting with our children can help them become emotionally healthy human beings.

What Dr. Perry said that day has been ingrained in my mind and heart and has become one of the most powerful motivators in my life, as a mother and teacher. In no uncertain terms, he said that the brain builds neurological connections every time we speak and interact with our children.

When we speak to our children, we are helping these connections to happen in the brain. What does this mean? Well, what it means is that every brain cell in our head wants to connect to another one. When we talk and interact with our children, these brain cells are connecting. Let me give you an example.

Let's say that you have a piece of good information you want to pass on to a friend. Well, you pick up the phone and dial your friend. Success! You got through and you are able to share the exciting information. Your friend becomes excited and decides that she will pass on the wonderful news, too. So, now she decides to call her sister and she tells her what is going on. Her sister does the same thing and now a wonderful chain of communication is established.

Each time someone calls, the information becomes more ingrained in everybody's lives until it becomes part of how they think and act. Well, this is no different with our children's language skills. The more they hear and interact in meaningful conversations with adults, the stronger these language connections will become. Each time a song is sung, the cells in the brain receive this information and make a stronger connection with each other.

These connections are important because we want our children's language receptors in the brain to be strong and healthy. Dr. Perry also said that by our playing and talking with our children, we help foster these brain connections that help students become ready for school. That is why he is a strong proponent of reading to children. When we read to our children, we help their brain development.

Dr. Perry's research has led him to see the types of behaviors that create healthy and strong individuals. His studies help teachers because he promotes language development through small and large interactions with our children. Remember that the strength of your child's language development will become a determining factor in how your child thinks and perceives his world. This development will automatically transfer itself to your child's academic success.

I hope you decide to look up Dr. Perry. Google him! You will be amazed by all his research. You Tube has quite a few videos on him. They are very educational and simple to understand. More importantly, his revolutionary ideas might help you change the way you view the role you play in your child's education.

As always, thank you for listening.
Lovingly,
Your child's teacher

LETTER 27

Putting Our Ideas Into Writing

Dear Parents,

I think it is time for me to explain how teachers take all these different concepts we have spoken about and incorporate them into writing. A good explanation should help make things easier for you to understand what goes on in the classroom when writing is taught. It will also help you become aware of what to look for in your child's writing.

So, let's review what we have learned so far. Writing is a skill that puts all of our thoughts into written form. The more exposure to language a child has, the easier it will be for him or her to learn how to write. Therefore, the development of language in the early years is crucial to the development of good writing.

More importantly, language development through conversations, games, and songs promotes thinking. The more fluent a child is in her thinking, the easier it will be for her to express herself and be understood, promoting good self-esteem and a sense of wellbeing within. The key person to promote language development in your child is you since you are the one who spends the most time with her. When children are spoken to regularly, they are better prepared for academic learning because we have helped their language development grow and flourish. The foundation becomes well-established.

Now that your child is expressing herself in an easy and fluent way, we teachers are able to begin teaching writing. There are different techniques we can use to foster writing, but teachers normally use a mixture of them because people learn using different modalities (ways of learning such as visual or auditory). We serve our students best when we incorporate these modalities because then our children will have different techniques to draw from as they get older.

We should also consider that through experimentation, children will find the modality that suits them best. Since we teachers cannot know what that will be because each child is unique, we try to present a good selection of writing and thinking techniques to help and encourage your child's written expression. However, the basis for all of the techniques is language development, which happens in the earlier years at home.

One of the methods teachers use is called "Whole Language." This method combines a set of skills together to produce writing. The skills it incorporates are listening, speaking, reading, and writing. This method really combines everything we have spoken of up to now. We first hear and process what is being said (listening), and then we are able to incorporate our thoughts through words (speaking). The verbal interchange helps us clarify what we are thinking. This clarification is followed by incorporating ideas and thoughts that are read to us or by us. Finally, we are able to express these concepts through the written form.

If the child is very young, she will scribble and then draw. This stage will be followed by labeling what she is illustrating. The labeling many times will be done by sounding out words. Children will sound out a word and write it out as it sounds to them. Do you remember the exercise we spoke about earlier in Letter 20 in which you help your child sound out words? Sounding out words is perfectly okay. It is called inventive spelling because the child is writing down the sounds she hears.

At this stage, it does not matter if she spells the word "cat" with a "C" or a "K." The point is that she is trying to write and is already thinking. As we progress, we will correct those invented spellings. Your child will learn all of the ins and outs of spelling and writing grammatically. What's important here is that we don't want to interrupt the thought process, which is what truly matters. If the thinking stops, because I am focusing on the spelling, I will send the wrong message ("You are not doing this well") and the thinking will stop due to the child's frustration or sense of humiliation. It is better to concentrate on the development of ideas and then begin to correct spelling, grammar, punctuation, and the like at a later time.

As the school year goes by, I will hand out spelling lists for your child to study. It is important that she actually studies these lists. When she is forced to learn how to spell these words through sounding them out, writing them three or five times every night, and writing a sentence with each one of them, then I am actually helping your daughter to retain information, recognize patterns in language and spelling, develop her vocabulary by enriching it, and build focus and stamina.

Yes, we develop stamina through studying! Finally, I am helping develop all of those tools that are necessary for her to express her ideas. Please remember those neurological connections I spoke of in Letter 26. When we teachers send homework home, we are helping to build these brain cell connections, which are what will help your child have strong thinking patterns. It is through practice that these patterns are developed. We need children to do their homework daily because it is the only way they will be able to reinforce these patterns and become proficient at what they are taught. Please help us by having your child do his or her homework.

Grammar plays a key role in proper writing. Language development helps with the expression of ideas. There is a direct connection between how you hear an oral expression and how you write it. If I am asked to explain my ideas, I will be able to hear myself speak. So if I say, "She talk fast," I realize immediately that it is not correct because I hear it.

We need to hear ourselves speak to be able to correct these natural mistakes. At first, young children make these types of grammatical errors as they speak. However, with constant interaction through conversations, they are able to correct them and realize the proper grammatical sequence of our oral language. This translation is related to writing. If we can't recognize grammatical oral patterns, this lack of recognition will be reflected in our writing because we write as we think.

One of the best ways to help our students correct their grammatical mistakes is by having them re-read what they wrote and pick out these mistakes by themselves. Let me show you through an example:

The boys walk to the park yesterday.

Do you see the mistake? Of course you do. The word "walk" should be in the past tense. The correct word should be "walked." The correct sentence should be: The boys walked to the park yesterday.

Think about this: How do you know the correct grammar form? Well, most likely because you hear it and recognize it. Some of you can tell me the actual grammar rule. The majority of us don't even know it. We just realize we can pick up on it. When you converse with your child, you are helping her structure her oral language properly. This oral structure transfers to writing.

Punctuation is important because it tells us where the natural pauses are in the written language. It also helps us define what is being said. If a child does not know where a sentence begins and ends, he will create a run-on sentence. You know, the type of sentence that never ends because the writer keeps adding ideas to it and all of them are tied together by an "and." An example of this type of writing would be:

I went to the park and played with my cousins and then we had lunch and then we played with the balls and then we had to get ready to go home and I asked my mommy if Johnny could come spend the night and she said it was okay.

You get my point. This is a very long sentence. If we want to make sense out of it, we need to break it down. It should look like this:

I went to the park to play with my cousins. After lunch, we played with the balls. When it was time to get ready to go home,

I asked my mommy if Johnny could spend the night. She said it was okay.

Teaching children where the natural breaks in language are is not an easy task. Teachers need to help students understand that a sentence has a subject (who or what we are talking about) and a predicate (what the subject is doing or what is being said about the subject). These are abstract terms in many cases because we don't see the subject or what it is doing. We have to picture it in our head. As I said before, this abstract idea is not easy to teach because many of our students are still developing their thought patterns. They need to see the concrete—in other words, what they can grasp. Here is where you come in. The more we converse with our children, the better they are able to imagine and picture abstract concepts in their heads. So when they begin to write, they are better equipped to do so.

I know this discussion is a very simple explanation of how teachers teach your child to write. However, it is just meant for you to understand what we do in school and how it requires your constant help. The partnership we share with you is fundamental to your child's academic development. You lay the foundation for what we do.

Without you, teachers struggle, because in many ways, you are the mortar that helps us cement all the different skills together. We teach skills and how to develop them, but you are the foundation for what your child is going to be like. You are the one who needs to practice with them.

Think about it.
Lovingly,
Your child's teacher

LETTER 28

Setting Up Expectations and the Will to Persevere

Dear Parents,

In my last letter, I mentioned homework and stamina. You were not sure what I was talking about and you asked me to clarify it for you. I am happy to do so.

Let's start with stamina. Stamina is the ability we all have to endure something. Let's say we want to run a five-mile race. We can't just get up and run the race, can we? We need to prepare to do so. This preparation means that we are aware of what our final goal is and we must decide on the best way to get there. So, we decide to start training for this race. We might start by running half a mile, and in a few days, we may decide we want to run an additional half a mile.

Little by little, we condition our body to endure the competition. In other words, we build stamina. It does not come easily; it requires patience and dedication. If we continue to practice and work at it, eventually, we will be able to achieve our goal. Imagine yourself running the race.

When we get an academic education, we go through a similar process. The thing is that we do not see the results right away because, most of the time, we are dealing with abstract concepts and what we can actually perceive is not always tangible. Yet, if we plan on being successful, we know that education plays an important role in our success. Reading, writing, and math are skills we all need to master if we plan on moving forward in life. The better our mastery, the easier things are for us.

So what does academic stamina look like? Well, it looks like persistence. When we try to persevere, we normally do not see much at first, but we do perceive small changes that will eventually combine to become part of a successful person. Now, please listen carefully; I am not defining someone as successful because he has a college degree and is making a lot of money. No, success is something else. It is the ability to be content with what one is doing. In many ways, it is feeling satisfied with one's accomplishments and what we are giving back to those around us. It is the knowledge that we can contribute to our society and know that our contributions are important.

The question that follows is: How do I develop academic stamina in my child? Well, it is quite easy to do if we are willing to put time into it. It will mean a bit of initial sacrifice and then constant monitoring until your child gets it. Yet, the nice thing is that once he gets it, your parenting will be much easier because you will have ingrained it into his system. As with everything, the initial cost is great, but the payoff is huge.

Think of your son going off to college and actually being ready for it. Now, think of him enjoying college and making the best of the academic success he is given. All of us want this success and sense of contentment for our child. It is only natural that we prepare him for college because a higher education is one of the many steps he might choose to master in the biggest picture of all—life.

Now, I have to say something that is important and that you may or may not agree with. College is not for everybody, but an education is. What do I mean by this? Well, not all students want to go to college or are ready for it. Some prepare themselves for life in other ways. Some of my students aspire to being dancers and empowering themselves and others through their movements. Other students choose technical careers where they work with their hands.

The point is that not all students have a calling to pursue rigorous academic training. Not all students want to work with abstract intellectual concepts most of their lives. The end result of people following different paths in life is that we have a beautiful group of individuals who can contribute to our society in their own unique ways. Howard Gardner, an author and developmental psychologist, tells us how people learn through different modalities, such as visual or auditory learning, and how students and individuals have different learning styles.

We are not all meant to fit one pattern. Yet, an academic education is important because it teaches us to read, write, speak, add, and subtract among many other skills. All of these skills are important when we talk about creating thinkers and individuals who contribute to our global society.

Having said that, it is time I explain one of the most important ingredients in developing academic stamina. It starts by setting a certain level of expectation for your child. The goal has to be realistic and accurate. An example is, "You will learn how to read and write well. By the time you finish high school; you will be reading at the expected level and be ready for college." If your child is not into academics, the goal could be: "You will finish high school and then go to a trade school to sharpen your skills." The need for this goal is very important because it establishes what you expect from your child. Remember, most students will try to raise themselves to the level of expectation you set because they want you to be proud of them.

Set the bar high and talk about it often. See how your child responds. It's important to talk with your child about reaching this goal. This conversation should be simple—please, no lecturing because that is a turn off. Instead, saying, "I saw your math grade was not that great. What happened? Is there something I can do to help?" will do. Place the responsibility on the child. He needs to know he is responsible for his grades and academic learning.

Think about it. If you don't, you are taking away an integral part of what it means for your child to be free—the need to understand his choices and their consequences. We need to let our kids experience failure every once in awhile if we expect them to be successful. We learn more from our failures than our successes. Please, let your child become accountable for a failed grade. It is the only way he will realize he needs to study more or work harder. These are valuable life lessons.

When we fail at something, we need to get back up and try again. And we need to teach our children the importance of doing the same. Maybe your child will try using a different approach, but it is necessary that he get back up. All successful people have experienced some type of setback in their lives; your child needs to overcome one as well.

When you have a setback at work, you are the responsible one, not your colleagues. If you let your children learn this lesson at school, you are providing them with a safe place to experience setbacks, and you are also providing them with the opportunity to learn how to get up when they are not successful.

These lessons are important, and we can only learn them through experiencing them. So raise the level high and make sure your child knows what that expectation is. Then talk about it often and provide the needed support.

I will let you think about this. In my next letter, I will explain the steps you can take to be successful at helping your child develop academic stamina.

Lovingly,
Your child's teacher

LETTER 29

Teaching Our Children Perseverance

Dear Parents,

 I am glad to see you have thought about the previous letter. The concern you have for your child's academic and social wellbeing is evident. I see how hard you are working at transforming some of your old thoughts and perceptions in order to help your child. As a teacher, my admiration for you grows. When we want to change someone, it starts by changing ourselves, and you are living proof of it.

 A few days ago, I read a book to some of my students. It was a children's version of Gandhi's life. As a class, we discussed how peace starts with us being quiet in our hearts. We decided that we can only change the world one person at a time, and the only person we can change is us. All of the children agreed with the idea that we have a little angel who reminds us to be good on one shoulder and another not so good angel on the other shoulder.

 It is up to us to decide whether or not we behave. We are the only ones who can decide for ourselves. Our conversation ended up being about making choices, and we agreed on one thing. When we make good choices, we help people change in positive ways and vice versa. In other words, we need to make sure that what we say and do is congruent. This is what I see you doing.

So, now that I have sung your praises, let me give you the magic formula for academic success. This formula has been around for many years. Many successful parents follow it, although only recently did I find the words to name it. I owe the actual labels to Ferney Ramirez, a psychologist who came to our school and did a series of presentations on parenting for the No Child Left Behind committee. I am thankful to him for giving me the words and sequence that transforms a norm into a way of acting and being.

When we decide we want to establish a routine, the best thing is to take something that is normal to us and transform it into a way of life. We all know how we can develop bad habits. We begin to do something constantly, and suddenly, it becomes a way of life. This magic formula is similar, but with the exception that we are working to create good habits within ourselves and our children. In many ways, we might be the ones who struggle initially because we are going to become very disciplined and consistent.

Please, don't let this process discourage you. I promise, in the end it will be worth it because your children will learn to follow routines automatically.

First, I want you to think of something you normally do on a regular basis. It might be making your bed every day as soon as you get up. Whatever it is, it is normal because you have been doing it for a long period of time. If you continue to do this activity constantly, without even thinking about, it becomes a norm. Norms are good because they mean that we do things normally—they are part of our set day. Well, when we have a certain norm we follow, day in and day out, it becomes a routine. Did you set it up on purpose? Most likely not, but it has become part of your routine.

Somehow or other, we internalize this routine as something that is comfortable to us. In many ways, we are creatures of habit and expect this routine in our day. When it is not there, we actually feel out of sorts because we need what is familiar to us. Suddenly, this routine has become a habit. We start acting without even thinking about it. Now, here is where the magic lies—your child is integrating his actions into his thinking. There is no questioning of what he does because there is congruency between what he thinks and his actions.

However, this congruency does not come easily; as a parent, you need to establish these routines carefully, but once you do… Magic! Your child knows what to do and does it without much of a struggle. The beauty is that at some point, he will internalize it and do it without you even having to remind him. Why? Well, this norm is so ingrained in his psyche that it has become a permanent way of thinking and acting!

Now how do you apply this norm to schoolwork? It is not difficult, but it will require consistent behavior on your part. In many ways, you will be retraining yourself. I don't know whether you have seen the television show *Supernanny*. On this show, the nannies teach the parents how to set a sorely needed routine for their children. If you have seen the show, you will see that the major modifications come from the parents. Once the parents establish the needed routine and boundaries, peace and tranquility begin to surface in the home.

Your home should be no different. You are the authority, so you need to establish the routine that will work best for your home. If you waver, your child will sense it and will be able to manipulate you with defying words and behaviors. That is something you don't want!

So how do we get started? Well, I will tell you what I did with my daughter and what I have told my sister to do. Please know that there is no one way to set a routine. You will have to find what works best for your home, yet the principles will remain the same. Cut yourself some slack and know you are an incredible person because you are daring to change yourself and some of your old habits in order to help your child. That deserves a round of applause. I am so proud of you!

The first thing to do is to set up a routine and tell your child what it will be. You want to verbalize it to your child because you want your child to internalize the routine as something that is normal and he can expect. The routine might look something like this: Every afternoon at four o'clock, your child sits down to do homework, even if your child is not at school. A toddler might sit down for ten minutes with you to read a book and then draw what he liked best from a story you just read him. Discuss it with him. The next day at four o'clock, you might play old-fashioned memory—after he reads another story, have him draw what he liked best about the story. This process has to be repeated over and over every day for a homework routine to be established. There should be no breaking the routine because you want it to stick and become something he internalizes so he starts doing it automatically. In other words, it is engraved in the way he acts and behaves. Creating this routine while your children are little helps them in the long run because the expectation is clear as they get older: "You need to do your homework well, and there are no buts or anything to disturb the routine. If you have no homework, you will sit and review math facts, read, or get ahead in an assignment. If nothing else, you will review what you are struggling with." Kids get it and don't argue because they are accustomed to this routine. Believe me, doing the work upfront saves hours of arguing later on.

Now the trick here is that you are teaching your child always to associate the same time of the day with doing homework. What is great about this routine is that, little by little, he will learn to sit still. He will also begin to learn how to focus and manage his own behavior. Remember, this change will develop very gradually, but it is achievable if you are consistent. Being consistent means that you follow this routine rain or shine, even when you have scheduled engagements.

At first, you will have to stick to this routine you are establishing so he learns to expect it as something that is normal. Once the routine is established, you can say, "We are going to Grandma's, but we still have to do our homework. Let's pack your coloring book and crayons so we can do it." At four o'clock, you will need to sit down with him. Maybe Grandma can sit with him instead so you get a well-deserved break. The main point is that he does not break the routine. Once things are going well, you might say, "Some weekends are a bit tough because we have a birthday party to go to. Should we do our homework before we leave?" Do you see what you are doing here? You are teaching responsibility and accountability. Your child is learning that he needs to fulfill his obligations before he can play. This situation is very similar to real life.

Finally, the day comes and your child enters preschool. The routine is the same. What will vary now is that your child will have to do his real homework. This might look like counting up to five and then matching the number with five little Cheerios.

Now that the school homework is done, do not let him go play, but finish off your routine. Why do I say this? Well, your goal is not to do homework and go play. You are looking for a routine; that is, a normal expected behavior that will then be integrated into the way he normally conducts himself. If you let him go play, you will see that he will start doing a sloppy job with his homework because he wants to get it over with so he can go play. This situation is not what you are aiming for. You want him to be able to concentrate and do things well and not rush through them. I had a little timer that I would set for my daughter. This timer indicated the amount of time she was to do homework and review. It was very successful because she realized that it is not only about handing in an assignment; it is about reviewing and getting into the habit of studying. This process was done very gradually and required a lot of persistence and patience on my part. It paid off.

Again, I understand that your child is little and you can't expect a whole hour of homework from him. However, you can expect a few more minutes than before because he has been building stamina. He should be able to sit a bit longer (not much, but a bit longer). As he gets older, his studying time will increase. The ideal amount of time for a first grader to do homework is about half an hour. This homework time should be used to study or review if homework was not given.

Sometimes, children finish quickly and want to go play. Instead, have them review a skill. If you need to, you can have them practice spelling words, reading fluency, adding or subtracting. There are many wonderful books with activities you can have them do. As they get older, they will associate this time with homework and study time. Yes, we do need to study. We all have to study and review what was taught. If we set up the routine early on, children will not struggle with it in future years.

I have just given you a lot of information. It might be best if you let it sink in and process it. We can talk more about setting up homework routines in our next letter.

Lovingly,
Your child's teacher

LETTER 30

Developing Responsibility and Discipline: Whose Job Is It?

Dear Parents,

Yes, you are right! The steps I described above are good for setting up any routine. They are crucial if we want to develop discipline. Please understand that discipline is not scolding and punishing. It is being taught how to self-monitor our own behaviors.

When we have learned to be disciplined, we choose to stay and fulfill our responsibilities before going out to play. Teaching our children the need to fulfill their obligations is crucial. As they get older, they will need to go to work and fulfill their duties. It is much easier to do so if they have developed a sense of commitment to their studies and other activities. Responsibilities will not feel so heavy to them.

This tool I just gave you will help you develop a sense of responsibility and discipline in your child. Many parenting books speak about developing a routine for your baby. This routine is necessary if you want to have a peaceful home. It also marks the difference in the level of stability your child feels. Why do I say this? Well, every single teacher strives to provide structure within your child's school day. It is the predictability of events that helps students enjoy a better day.

Teachers establish norms and routines starting the first day of school. It normally takes about a month or two to get things running in a predictable way. One of the first things we do is establish the rules that need to be followed. However, in many cases, these rules should be a continuity of what you are already teaching at home.

Simple things, such as taking turns when we talk, are some of the rules that are important in the classroom. Now, why do I say it is a continuity learned at home? Well, if you have conversed with your child, your child knows that there is a time to speak and a time to listen. Understanding these differences are part of your child learning to be respectful toward herself, her classmates, and her teacher. Yet, when children are not accustomed to these types of interactions, they struggle to focus on what others say and have a much harder time following the lesson that is being presented. These children will normally get bored, start fidgeting, and get themselves into trouble.

Are these "bad kids"? No, they are not! They simply have not had the benefit of learning how to sit through conversations and follow them. It clearly affects their learning. Remember, these children are smart; they just need a bit of help learning how to dialogue. Conversation is a skill that needs to be nurtured and developed. When we do so, we are able to hear what the other person is saying and our understanding grows. The lack of this skill affects your child's academic performance. I see this situation all the time.

Now, some of you might say it is the teacher's responsibility to teach this skill. And yes, we do try to teach it as best we can, but the true development of this integral skill is developed at home. We can only build on the platform you have established. Help us make the base of this platform rock-solid. If you do, my fellow teachers and I will have more time to teach because we will have to spend less time trying to manage behavior issues. It takes one kid to mess up a whole classroom.

Please think of some of the children you have seen on TV shows like *Supernanny* who struggle to behave. They are not easy for adults to handle, and their behavior is an indication that they feel the world that surrounds them is not there to support them. This is a sad statement. We as parents, teachers, and society have to help our students. Helping them is not the responsibility of one of these groups—it is the responsibility of all of us.

This situation reminds me of a conversation I had a few years ago. I was sitting in a person's kitchen and the kids in the house were out of control. The person's justification for their behavior was a simple one: "I work very hard to send my kids to a private school and look at how my kids are behaving. What is the teacher doing? I don't know why she has not been able to teach them how to behave." I promise you, that moment was one of the few times in my life when I didn't know what to say.

I was stunned, partly because I loved this person and the children who were surrounding me, and partly because part of parenting is educating our children so they can go to school and get an academic education. But education is much more than academics! It starts at home; it always has and always will. There is no exception. What parents do at home makes the biggest difference in their children's lives.

I think that for now, I will leave you with this idea. Was this person right? Is it the teacher's sole responsibility to teach her students to behave, or is she the person who helps the parents by reinforcing the good behavior that they have taught at home? Should the teacher be teaching a parent's kids how to behave? Whatever your answer might be, you should be able to justify it to yourself. Please think about it. As you try to answer this simple question, you will gain a deeper knowledge of yourself and what you believe.

In many ways, my request that you try to answer this question is similar to an exercise I would give to your child. Yet, if we had not established all of the previous background information, we would not be able to have an honest discussion. These types of exercises are meant to help us grow and develop as parents and, most importantly, as human beings. I will leave you with your thoughts for now.

In our next letter, we will discuss our findings.

Thank you for being you and being brave enough to follow your own convictions.

Lovingly,
Your child's teacher

LETTER 31

Educating vs. Teaching— The Value of Following Through

Dear Parents,

In our last letter, I asked you to think about education and the role parents play in it. Here is what I got out of your answers. First of all, we have been talking about teaching our children life skills that help us to educate our children. We build these skills little by little with a lot of patience and dedication. They do not come easily to us or our children. Yet through continuous modeling and repetition of our own behavior and our expectations, we educate our children.

Most of us think that teaching and educating are the same thing, but they are not. They both are part of the same coin—one is heads and one is tails—and yes, they are definitely intertwined, but let's not assume they are the same because they are not.

There is a distinction between teaching and educating. I want to discuss this distinction with you because it will make a big difference in how we, in the teaching profession, can help your child become successful.

So what is teaching? In its simplest form, teaching is showing someone how to do something. It is that easy. You teach someone how to make a sandwich, how to dust, how to mop, or how to read. We are all teachers; every single one of us is a teacher. If we are good at explaining and modeling a skill, we can be quite successful. In the olden days, many people were apprentices of a blacksmith, a shoe cobbler, a tailor, etc. People taught other people a skill. If the person was quick, he would pick up on it and be able to repeat the skill with ease and carry on.

This type of teaching does not constitute an education. An education is much more than learning skills. An education combines, integrates, and develops all of these skills into an integral part of who we are. In other words, the skills become part of our character. They begin to take on a life of their own as we learn to value them. In many ways, these skills become a huge part of who we are and what we value. They become apparent in how we behave, in how we express ourselves, and in our ideas and ideals. Only then can we say they are part of our education.

So an education is not only what we learn at school. It is a combination of what is taught and modeled at home and then at school. The biggest part of our child's education comes from home. The values children acquire or don't acquire are a reflection of what is being taught at home. These lessons can be positive or negative and intentional or unintentional. Let me explain with an example.

As parents, we constantly remind our children to do their homework. We tell them that their homework is important because it will help them learn and get a better job in the future. Yet we are too busy trying to earn a living and spending a lot of time at work to help them with it. When we get home, we ask whether the homework is done. What a silly question; of course, it is done. So we do not check to see whether it is done.

As parents, we believe we are teaching our children the importance of being responsible. We also believe we are teaching them that an education is important for improving our lot in life because we ask whether their homework is done. Our intentions are good ones, and we are doing the best we can. Nobody can question our intentions and the love we have for our children. Yet, we are not really teaching these lessons to our children. They hear our words, "An education is important; that is why you need to do your homework," but those are only words.

To make our words meaningful, truly meaningful, we have to follow through with our actions. "Okay, let me see your homework. Let's review it. Okay, I see you have this correct, but this seems to be incorrect. What do you think you need to do to improve it? How can you fix it?"

Following through is such an integral and difficult part of educating our children. When we ask our children whether the homework is done and do not follow through, we are teaching them that they are not accountable. Therefore, we are saying one thing and doing another. There needs to be congruency between our words and our thoughts. Our children are magnets; they pick up on the lack of congruency we exhibit in our behavior. What they see is an easy way out. "Mom and Dad don't check or don't care, so why should I?" When children see this, they don't practice their academic skills. The skills have been taught, but without practice and review, your children won't get far in learning them. Practice and review are what make a lesson stick—nothing else.

So let's go back to what we are intentionally and unintentionally teaching our children. All of us have good intentions; we want our children to value an education. Yet, when we don't follow through, we are unintentionally teaching our children that we really don't value education because we are not being congruent.

Ultimately, we are missing a key ingredient in our equation: following through. The lack of following through in our actions is the one thing our children always pick up on. When they become aware through our actions of what we truly stand for and what we don't, they get mixed signals. They know that what we say and do are very different things, so they have a lot of leeway to slide by. Your help is crucial to us, the teachers. Please think about the following…

"How does what I just learned apply to my child's academic education?" You tell me. Please analyze and think about this question. I can tell you, but as a good teacher who wants your help, I know it is best for you to think about it. We will come back to this subject again. It is inevitable.

As always, thank you for listening to me.
Lovingly,
Your child's teacher

LETTER 32

Teaching Perseverance Through Homework

Dear Parents,

You searched and found your answers. You say you realize you don't always follow through. How can you when you are not sure how to do so? You say it is hard because you are tired after working a long day; when you try to push through with some type of continuity for your children, it becomes a battle and you prefer to back down. Bad habits seem to have taken hold of your home.

You asked me to give you some tips. As always, I promise I will do my best. Please remember that you will need to modify some of these. They are suggestions that have worked for some parents and can work for you as long as you modify them to your own home environment.

Nowadays, most people seem to have so many distractions. Let me explain. When your child sits down to do his homework, what is going on at home? Is your nephew visiting and wanting to play? Is the TV on? Is the radio or computer available to your child? Most likely, one of these options is the cause of distraction. Your child can't concentrate and focus because his attention is being called elsewhere. So when your child is doing his homework, there should be no distractions.

The TV, iPod, radio, and computer should be off. By off, I mean that not even you are watching the TV if it provides a distraction to your child. "What? Even the computer?" Yes, even the computer. Most children do not need the computer to do their homework. As a matter a fact, it becomes a huge distraction for the majority of them because they will start surfing the net and chatting with their friends. They will be switching on and off from one screen to another and not necessarily studying.

Remember, studying requires a quiet and concentrated effort and focus. Electronic gadgets become distractors instead of aids to studying in most cases. (One of the exceptions will be when children do research for their assignments. We can discuss that at another time.)

A few years ago, a parent complained to me about the amount of homework I gave his daughter. He said it would take her up to four hours to get it done. I asked whether she sat in a quiet space to do it. He said she didn't. It seems the TV was always on and the whole family would be watching it while she was doing her homework. It was obvious to me why she took so long to get it done. There were constant interruptions. She was not able to concentrate and review what had been taught in class that day. No wonder she was doing poorly in class.

Let me explain to you what is the function of homework. Homework provides an opportunity to review what was taught by the teacher that day. It is a review in which the student needs to sit down by herself and practice what was learned. This review is crucial to learning because the child will evaluate what it is that she understood and what she didn't. This self-awareness is important because your child is beginning to self-monitor, asking herself, "What do I know? What do I need to go over?" In other words, your child begins to be accountable for her own learning. Accountability is very important for success. When we do not provide this learning space for her, she might miss out on a very important lesson in life—accountability.

Yes, children, even young ones, need to know they are accountable for their own learning. We cannot ask them to perform properly if they do not feel a sense of accountability for their own education. Education then becomes this thing they have to do that is boring and a chore. Yet, when they understand that they are going to school because they will learn new things and will be able to make a difference in their world and that of others, they are given a goal—something to strive for.

Children need to see that the benefits they receive from an education are much more than just being able to get a paycheck in the future. Our attitude is what will show them this. So when your child brings homework home, remember there is a reason for this homework being sent. Maybe the teacher has sent home a review because the whole class is struggling with a concept. The teacher might need the students to become better at recalling facts or understanding a concept. Re-reading is important because if we read carefully, we will gain a deeper knowledge of what is being said to us.

Do you know why children need to watch a movie over and over again? It is because they are trying to gain a deeper understanding of the concepts being presented to them. Children need this repetition in order to learn. It is no different in school. Children need to practice what they have learned, and homework provides this repetition for them.

Remember the wiring of the brain? When your child practices, she is rewiring the connections that will become the basis for a different type of learning. Reviewing creates the opportunity for students to learn and expand their knowledge. In his book *The Social Animal*, David Brooks talks about children who work hard at problem solving. These children will normally be able to perform better on a standardized test. He gives an example of a person taking a test; the longer the person is able to concentrate and work out the intricacies, the better she will do.

Many times, we see students easily give up because they have not developed the ability to stick with something and follow through with it. A very good example is when the students take standardized tests. I can't begin to tell you how many times a child bubbles in the whole test without reading the questions. As a teacher, all I can do is suggest that the child review it. The whole thing is beyond frustrating because the child has not tried at all. Why does this situation happen? Because many (not all) students do not have a sense of how to work things out. This process is difficult, so they give up before they have even started. In other words, they have not developed the work ethic they need to carry them forward in life. So again, teachers can teach and provide the necessary homework to develop this skill, but it really comes down to you, the parent. Can you provide that structured time, without interruptions, to your child? It is necessary if you want your child to have the stamina and ability to follow through. This ability is essential.

Remember, it is the daily consistency that will allow your child to develop these character traits. At a party, a mother asked me why we sent homework packets for the whole week. She just thought they were a nuisance and preferred to get them done on the weekend. This plan might sound smart. The chore is then done, and there is no struggling with the child during the week.

But is this mother teaching her children the value of everyday consistency? Is she teaching them the value of perseverance? Is she really letting her children work out the small glitches they will encounter with the homework? No, she is not. Is she relegating the homework to the weekend because she does not care? No, she is a mother who cares deeply about her children and finds that helping with homework on the weekend has worked best for her. So when I explained the reasoning behind the homework packets, she started to change things around. After that, her children began to do much better in school, and not surprisingly, they have started to become more independent. She likes that!

So please think about how important homework is for your child's development. Maybe these ideas are new to you. They should be. Most of the time, teachers don't explain this concept to parents. Now you know that you and I can begin to change some things in order to help your child. Nobody said parenting was easy. Yet, as always, I am deeply moved by the commitment you have to your children. Thank you for being a reminder to me of what love for our children can do. It truly can move mountains.

Lovingly,
Your child's teacher

LETTER 33

Finding Strength to Set Boundaries

Dear Parents,

The ideas seem good to you. They seem logical and not too difficult to apply to your children, if they are little. However, they are not working that well with your older kids; after all, they have the ability to be much more defiant. Wow, do I know that! Yet, there is a remedy for this behavior.

You might not fully understand what I am going to ask you to do at first, but please do it. Doing so will give you the strength to confront your children without wavering, and they will understand that you will hold your ground no matter what.

Once your children see you mean business and that you are a united front with your partner, things will change drastically. However, you must be brave and hold your ground. Do not budge. Children sense when they can outmaneuver you. And if they smell a bit of guilt, they will use it against you. They are not mean, but they want to keep the status quo. Just like with us adults, they find it is easier to continue with things as they are, especially if they are not asked to put too much effort into maintaining the status quo.

We all fight change because it is scary. Yet for true transformation to happen, we need to change our old patterns, and because we are the adults, it is up to us to help change our children's old habits if we want to create a better future for all of us. Don't be afraid; you have come so far. I truly admire you. I have told you that several times, but it is true.

You are a continuous reminder to me of what is good and wonderful about human beings. The choices we make are what alter our lives and the lives of those we love. You are amazing; you truly are.

So, when we have older kids who have not been able to turn their behaviors into a norm and then into a routine and so forth, we need to teach them how to do so. How you teach it will depend solely on you. Remember, I will give you the general ideas, but it is up to you to adapt them to your home.

Before I give you this information, I need to ask you to think about something. Please, be as honest as you can in your answer. You are the only one who will know what your answer is, and it will make a difference in how you proceed. It is preferable that you answer this question first because it will help you figure out what your triggers are. Once you are aware of what they are, it will be harder for you to be triggered by your children's actions. Awareness will become your greatest ally when you need to stand your ground with your children.

Please imagine the following scenario: You are talking to a friend about how you are struggling with your child. Your child constantly leaves messes all over, and you truly are upset. Last night, you had a huge screaming match with your son because you got home and found a mess. The kitchen was dirty and things were not picked up. The laundry you had left folded and ready to put away is still there, and now you have to wash it again because the dog has been rolling all over it. You turn to see your child just sitting there, listening to music and chatting on his computer.

Suddenly, you feel your blood curdling and you explode. You are not even sure why you react this way. Looking back over the night's events, you are not sure what happened, and you realize that the dishes and the laundry are important, but not enough for you to have had such a huge reaction. Truly, what happened inside you? The answer to this question is what we need to discover. When we are able to understand our triggers, we can get a better grasp on things and help ourselves and our children. Learning what triggers us and how to prevent it will be hard work and it won't be easy, but it will get you to a better place. I promise.

So, back to our scenario; you wake up the following morning and feel badly about what happened. Guilt makes you cringe, but so does anger. Who does this little punk think he is? After all, you are working your heart and soul out to provide a better life for him, but he has no consideration for you. Really, who does he think he is? The sense of entitlement is just too much, and no gratitude is ever shown for what you do. Very seldom do you hear, "I love you, Mom and Dad" or "Thank you for all you do."

So why should you keep going and giving to this person who does not show much gratitude? Well, because you love this child of yours. This person, this human being, no matter how annoying and ungrateful, is your child and you can't help but love him. When you have this realization, suddenly, you are filled with guilt. This is no ordinary guilt. Oh, no! This guilt is the kind that grips you in the stomach and makes you feel terrible because you perceive yourself as being out of control. After all, you have created this child. He is only behaving and acting the way you have unconsciously taught him to. What are you going to do?

The worst part is that when this situation happens, we are not sure why we exploded. We normally let things slide; what made it different this time? Consumed with guilt, we go watch TV to try to numb ourselves.

Does this scenario sound right? To some of us, it might be all too familiar. Others might not experience something so drastic, but I can guarantee we have all had something similar happen. It is a reality that too many of us have confronted as parents. We end up asking ourselves, "What am I doing? Is it right or not? I am trying my best, but I just don't know if I'm truly guiding my child in the right direction." All these questions and doubts are experienced by all parents.

We are only human. More importantly, we have all exploded at some point or other. The question is: Why? Answering that question is my homework to you.

Try to analyze why the parent in our short scenario exploded. Truly try to get into that parent's psyche and help him understand. Is it really the laundry and the dishes, or is it something else? If it is something else, what is it? You see, in these questions, you will find answers to why you explode or give up without a fight. Remember, we talked about the different levels of thinking. Well, this time I am asking you to apply them to yourself.

You will need to analyze the whole story. Maybe you will find yourself comparing it to something all too familiar. Whatever your answers are, they will help you to understand yourself better as a person and a parent. Many of us experience some behavior or attitude from somebody and feel our blood rush, but we are not sure why.

Understanding will help to prepare you to hold your ground in a loving and caring way with your child. That is what we are striving for.

I will leave you to think about this question for now. However, as soon as you let me know what your thoughts are, I will be happy to listen and converse with you.

Lovingly,
Your child's teacher

LETTER 34

Taking Control by Setting Good and Functional Boundaries

Dear Parents,

Wow! That exercise was rough but necessary. Please know I did something similar once and I know it was hard. Yet, it was very fruitful because I learned a lot about myself. The knowledge I gained empowered me to become a better person and a better parent. I began to analyze my little home scenarios closely and started to become aware of what I was feeling at a certain moment. I still analyze them whenever I feel a trigger because it is empowering for me. I need to try to be in a good place emotionally when I confront my children, and that is where I want you to be as well.

Now, let me recap what you said. The anger the person in the scenario experienced was not really about the dishes or clothes. You realized that the dirty kitchen and laundry were the trigger to something that had been festering for a while—not being appreciated. Yet, you are not sure why this person exploded on this particular day but other times just let things slide. Why?

You thought it might be because this individual was very tired, hungry, or just annoyed by a bad experience at work. The thing this parent was craving was a bit of peace and quiet, and instead, the parent found a mess. You also mentioned that maybe the child could have helped pick up the mess instead of listening to music and chatting. After all, this child does live in the house and can and should contribute. To sum it all up, the explosion was about not feeling appreciated and feeling that he or she is taken for granted.

You are right; most of the things we say or hear have a deeper meaning. The problem is that we focus on what is being presented on the surface because that is what is being pointed out. People sometimes think it is no big deal because, after all, it is only the dishes. Yet, what is really stirring up all those feelings is bubbling, and we don't know what it is or how to say it.

Finding out what really triggers us is what is important, and it's also important to explain it to our child so he can understand why we feel the way we do. This discussion allows us to relate to each other. Our children need to understand that we also have feelings and struggles and that we are doing the best we can. We might not always get it right. We don't need to. As long as our child sees we are trying, there will be a better reception to what we are saying, and that is why I had you do the previous exercise. If you can confront your child with honesty and love, your opportunity for success will be greater.

So here we go. When you have a child who is in her pre-teens or early teens, you need to set certain parameters of behavior—in other words: expectations. These expectations need to be clear, very clear. Let me give you an example:

"Honey, the kitchen needs to be picked up by 6 p.m. when I get home from work. This means that the dishes will be washed and put away. You will also make sure that the kitchen counters have been wiped down and all the crumbs are not on the floor. Make sure you sweep. I know that you will do a good job and this will allow me to cook dinner quickly so we can enjoy watching our show afterwards."

Is this example clear? Yes! It says what you need to have done, how you expect it to be done, and by when. More importantly, you are letting your child know why you need it done and what will happen after dinner.

The reward or consequence will be watching a show together. At first, you might have to show your daughter what your expectations look like, so you teach her how to clean up the kitchen. You might have to show her where to put away things and how to wipe off the counters. If your daughter is like mine, she might take a dirty rag and wipe off the counter. I don't like it that way. Instead, I have to show her first how to scrub the counter with a bit of soap and then wipe it off with a dry rag. Then she needs to take a wet rag and wipe off all the soap and finally dry it off with a clean towel. Picky, I know, but my daughter has no doubt now of what is expected because I showed her.

Let's now say that you come home from work after you have told your child your expectations, but the kitchen is not picked up. Don't get mad—at least, try not to show it. Very calmly, state the following, "I asked you to pick up the kitchen and you chose not to." Yes, it was your child's choice. "This is unfortunate because now I will have to wait for you to pick up before I can start cooking. Cooking dinner will take a while, and we most likely will miss the show."

You are going to make a point in taking forever to cook dinner. You will make sure dinner is not ready until the show is on. Therefore, your child can't watch it because you are finishing cooking and she will have to help with some of the prepping for dinner. Find extra chores for her to do if you need to. The point is that she now understands you mean business. My daughter and her friends say that the bad thing about me is that I don't mind embarrassing myself if it proves my point. They are right, and therefore, they normally don't mess with me.

If this is the first time you have to confront your daughter in this manner, chat with her as things are getting done. "I see you are washing the dishes first. That is a good idea because that will free up the sink for me to start rinsing off the meat." Take your time. Put the meat in the sink and then decide you have to use the washroom. Remember you are stalling to make a point. The thing is, don't be too obvious. In many ways, you will be using the same tactics your child uses on you.

Let's say your daughter turns on the TV and starts watching it. Go turn it off. If need be, stand next to it until she goes back to the kitchen and starts doing what she needs to do. If she chooses not to cooperate and goes to her room, cook dinner for yourself and your family, but don't let her partake in it. Tell her, "Honey, the mess is still there and you have not done your share of the family work. We are a family and we all need to contribute to its wellbeing." She might decide to go get a snack. Go lock the snacks in the car and keep the keys on you. I normally keep very few snacks in the house. Most of the snacks are apples, cheese, crackers, etc. The kids don't gravitate to them unless they are really hungry, and I feel good about the choices I provide them.

Now you might say that this kind of discipline is cruel. Is it? Taking control of your house and showing your kids who is boss is not cruel. It is called "tough love," and if you set the tone for one kid, the others will get the point and follow suit. In many ways, you are killing two birds with one stone. That is good parenting.

Some kids will answer back and try to pick a fight. Do not let them snare you into a verbal argument. Children will trigger you consciously and unconsciously. That is why I had you do the previous exercise. All of these defiant behaviors are triggers of some sort or other. They affect us all in different ways. Some of us will have a stronger reaction than others. It is important that we keep our cool if we want to be successful. If we react harshly and say, "Forget it; there is no TV for you now," it sounds punitive and vindictive. You did to me; now I do to you. However, if you identify your triggers and try to stay as calm as possible, when you speak and act, your words will have a different tone to them. This tone is very important because it will convey a sense of disappointment in your child's decisions, but not in your child, herself. This difference is huge because you are judging her actions, not her.

This concept, I believe, needs further clarifying. It is not the same to say, "You are so dumb. Look at what you did," and "You must have not been thinking when you did that." There are two very different ways of judging the same action. One criticizes the person while the other one casts a judgment on the person's behavior. We need to try always to focus on the behavior. If we do, we are giving our child a way out, a way to improve. All of us make mistakes, and all of us need to find a way back from those mistakes. One way to do so is by correcting the negative behavior. Isn't that what we ultimately want?

There is a movie I love because it teaches us how to confront our children. It is the best and most powerful example of a confrontation I have ever seen. I will tell you about it in our next letter.

For now, I will leave you to think about all of this information.

Lovingly,
Your child's teacher

LETTER 35

Teaching Through Consequences and Confrontation

Dear Parents,

I am sorry. You did not like the cliffhanger I left you with. You wanted me to tell you the name of the movie, but I didn't. Maybe I should have told you, but I was afraid you would not have thought things over first. Sometimes, it is better to wait a bit and know that something good is coming. That's my true reason.

In our last letter, we spoke about confrontations. They are difficult and unpleasant, under any circumstances. Yet, they are unavoidable and are part of life. We can choose to have a huge screaming match or we can choose to try to stay calm, providing a good example of problem solving for our child. Children will have ample opportunities at school and in life to try out whatever we choose to model for them as a source of conflict resolution. Let's try and give them the best model we can.

Therefore, I want to present you with another idea. Many of us struggle with our kids studying. We can't seem to get them to study because they find it too hard to focus. You had not used any of the previous methods because you were not aware of them. Instead, you bribed. Teachers see this all the time at school. "My dad and mom said that if I get straight A's, they will buy me the computer game I want." This reward or "bribe" seems like a good incentive, but it isn't. Let me tell you why.

First of all, you are opening yourself for bigger presents every time. When does enough become enough? If we have to give our child something every time he does something, we are taking away from him the opportunity to do something just because it is the right thing to do.

We study because it is important to learn, and it will provide us with ways to empower ourselves, not because everything we do deserves a reward. If we constantly reward, we are creating children who are self-centered and truly entitled. This is not what we want. Think of Dudley in the Harry Potter books. On his birthday, he had thirty some presents, but he was mad and outraged because it was one less than the previous year. You do not want your child to turn out like that; nobody does. You want your child to be appreciative of what he gets and to see the effort and thought you put into it. More importantly, the biggest reward is the education itself. Many things we do in life are done because they need to be done—not because a big prize is going to be given to us.

The question we need to answer is: What should you do? Well, first of all, remind yourself that you are the parent, and therefore, the person in charge. You are the one who pays the bills, and that means you have enormous power over your children. They are dependent on you and they know it. By now, they also know that you won't accept emotional guilt as easily and that your triggers are diminishing. You are taking control, and there is not much they can do about it. So, now we are ready to start laying down our rules. I will provide you with an example since that always seems to work best. Then we will analyze it and pinpoint the key points.

Let's say your daughter needs a computer to do her science research. Your old computer is slow and freezes up quite a bit. There seems to be a need for a new family computer. So, you do your own sleuthing and find a good computer for your family. Before you go buy it, you need to set the rules. They will be set in steel; that means there is no wavering on your part. Here is what the discussion, preferably with both parents contributing, should sound like:

"Honey, we will be buying a new computer for the family. Your father and I [always a united front] realize that you are beginning to do more research and it is necessary for you to complete your assignments. However, we are going to set some very clear rules for this computer. By following them, you will gain access to the computer. If you choose not to follow them, you can always use the public library computers."

"Mom! Dad! That's not fair!"

"We are not asking if it seems fair or not. We are giving you these rules because they are the ones that work best for our home."

"But—"

"These are the rules. Our first rule is that the computer will stay in the family room."

"But—"

"You will be able to use it for your research while everybody is reading and doing homework. We will continue to do homework in the family room from four to six."

"But that is not fair."

"Honey, as we said before, this is not about fair; it is about what works best for our home. Your mother and I need to know you are doing your homework and need to be able to help you if you need it."

"I'm not a baby. I can do my homework on my own."

"We agree, yet our decision stands."

"The second rule is that you will use the computer after you do all of your reading and math homework. Most of the time, you don't need it for those assignments."

"I am not a baby."

"We know you are not, and as a young lady, you are capable of understanding the rules. You will choose to follow them if you plan on using the computer."

"But—"

"When you are researching, you will stick to your research. You will not be chatting with friends on the computer."

"That's unfair!"

"As we said, these are our rules. Fair or not, these are our rules. Finally—"

"There's more?"

"Yes, there is more. Once you have done your homework and finished all of your responsibilities, you will be able to play with the computer for an hour. This will be your free time with the computer. This is when you will be able to chat, play games, and surf the web for whatever interests you."

"Finally!"

"Do you understand the rules?"

"Well, do I have a choice?"

"No, there are no choices. Take our offer or leave it. So, what is it going to be?"

"I guess it is okay."

"Both of us are glad to see you have chosen to abide by the rules. One last thing—if you choose to break the rules, you are telling us that you are not interested in using the family's computer and we will respect your choice. The computer then will be off limits until you have proven, to yourself and us, that you are ready to use it responsibly."

"Okay!!!"

"We are glad to see you understand. Now let's go buy the computer."

This long dialogue represents a perfect scenario. You are confronting your daughter in a very matter of fact way. You are presenting your argument (reasons) without wavering and she knows it. There is no room for her to try to outmaneuver you. More importantly, you are spelling out the rules. They are very clear and there is no space for "I thought." The argument is tight and logical. She is also able to be given a choice, follow the rules, and receive the benefits they provide—use of the computer. If she chooses not to follow the rules, she only has herself to blame. Wow! That is teaching consequences and accountability. There is nobody to blame but herself.

Now, let's say you bought the computer and things are going well. However, one day you catch your daughter breaking the rules. She has started to chat and play games on the computer while doing her homework, therefore, not focusing on her homework or doing a good job. What do you do? First, you should confront her calmly.

"May I know why you chose to break our agreement?"

"Mom, I already finished my homework."

"I see; you are finished and you thought you could use this time to chat with your friends."

"Yes."

"I see. However, your father and I were very clear about our rules, weren't we?"

"Yes."

"Okay. Now, let me be very clear on this. We agreed that you would let us know when you didn't want to use the computer by breaking the rules. Is that correct?"

"Well…I guess…Yes!"

"I thought so."

"Mom, but I have an assignment due by next Friday."

"I see. Do you need me to take you to the local library? You can research there while I look for some books I have been meaning to read. Get your stuff; it will also be a nice break for me."

Some of you might say this is drastic. Is it? Think about this: Are the mother's responses cruel? Are they mean-spirited? Furthermore, is the mother acting out of spite? No, she isn't. She is trying to teach her daughter that certain behaviors have consequences. The earlier the daughter learns this, the better it will be for her. The consequences aren't mean either. The mother is not telling her daughter that she doesn't care. She is actually taking her to the library, thereby providing a solution to the problem. Maybe tomorrow she will just drop her off instead of staying at the library with her. Yes, there will be several days without a computer for the daughter. She will need to go to the library. You ask why the library instead of a friend's house? Well, a friend's house is a privilege, isn't it? Are you going to punish and then reward? No, you need to be consistent. After the assignment is finished and turned in, you can give her a new opportunity to use the home computer again. You can make the offer by saying:

"Honey, I see you finished your project. Your mother and I are very proud of you. Well done. We were wondering if you might want to try following the computer rules one more time. You have been responsible; you chose to make the best out of a difficult circumstance, and we believe that shows maturity on your level. So, what do you say?"

"Okay."

This dialogue may seem unreal to some of you. Yet, it is achievable. It will all depend on you. You can do this. It won't happen overnight because it takes time and patience. But it can be done. The secret is not to give up and to keep at it. Stick to the rules agreed upon. Use the tools, and suddenly, you will become an expert at confronting your child in a loving way.

Watch the movie *Master Harold...and the Boys*. In it, you will find the best way to confront a teenager or young adult. If you choose to watch the movie, which I hope you do, you will find many tips to help you confront your child when you find yourself in a difficult situation. Listen to the dialogues carefully because they provide good examples of how to speak to our loved ones in a loving but firm way. Sam, one of the characters, will be the one you should listen to and watch. His character is full of loving wisdom, even when faced with difficult and unfair circumstances.

You will find many parallels between the example Sam conveys in this film and my writing. View it; buy it if need be. The point is that this movie will always be able to provide good insight in dealing with difficult teenagers and young adults. Be patient with the movie since most of it is dialogue. It is in these dialogues that I hope you find your strength; watch as Sam confronts with the truth and leaves the door open for dialogue. Creating this honest dialogue with your child is the secret. It is what I hope you can learn to do.

As you know, the school year has come to an end and I will miss you. I hope this movie can pick up for you where I have left off. Goodbyes are not easy for me, but it is time your children move on to a new adventure, and I will be here watching them go. Yet, I am comforted by all the growth I have seen in them and in you. I can't begin to tell you how proud I am. You took the biggest challenge—transforming yourself—in order to help your child. In my eyes, there is no greater sign of love or caring.

As I said in the beginning, we can only hope to transform ourselves. It is through this transformation that we can always see a silver lining of hope and love. Thank you, thank you for letting me be a part of your child's life and yours. More importantly, thank you for being my silver lining. Together, we make a difference.

Lovingly,
Your child's teacher

FINAL NOTE

As we come to the end of this school year, I see your child leave my classroom, and I am truly sad. I have grown to love him or her, and it is hard to let go. I know I will see your child, next year, in a different classroom. The thing is that it won't be mine anymore, and I will miss the smiles and love notes, the sticky hands and the hugs, the loud voices and the excitement of discovery. I have to remind myself that every school year brings joy and happiness with it. I have seen growth and much learning. This is your child's gift to me, and for that, I am thankful. It has been a great year.

However, this year my heart is full of joy for another reason. You see, you have come into my classroom; you stopped being a parent and became a friend. You became such an important part of our daily routines and dialogues. Yes, you did, even when you were not with us. You were present when little Johnny spoke about his weekend, you were present when Suzy shared at circle time, and you were present in your child's ideas and writing. Your child discovered his or her voice. It came out loud and clear in the class discussions because there was confidence in what was said. That confidence would have been lacking if you had not shared your ideas the previous night with your child. You have become such an integral part of my classroom that I am sad to see you go, and I wonder how you are going to continue to use the tools you learned this year.

You see, you have come so far. Do you remember when you would ask me, "What am I to do?" You didn't want anybody to know how lost you felt. You were afraid people would judge you. Yet, you decided that you would work hard to improve yourself and your family. Wow! What courage it took. You should be proud of yourself. I know I am. The question now is: How are you going to continue this growth? How are you going to continue to implement all of these strategies and life skills you have learned? Your home life and family need you to continue on this path. You can't stop now!

Please let me suggest one last thing. Take a few moments and write down all the successes you have experienced this year. Yes, write them down because when you feel things are getting rough, you will be able to look at them and know you are strong and can continue on this journey. Now, don't forget; post them some place where you can see them often. Mine are hanging on my closet door. Now, here comes the hard part—take a moment to identify what areas you need to continue to work on. I know this is not an easy task. There always seems to be room for growth. Look at those areas carefully because they will become your guiding compass. Are you ready for what comes next? Write a plan. It does not have to be an elaborate plan. Write down the ten action items you think will help you to continue on this successful journey. Here are ten lines for you to jot your thoughts down:

1. _____
2. _____
3. _____
4. _____
5. _____
6. _____
7. _____
8. _____
9. _____
10. _____

Oh, you want me to review what we learned? I will be happy to if it is going to help you create your action plan.

Let's see; we learned so many things:

1. **You learned how to communicate with your child.** You discovered that listening is a skill that requires time and patience to develop. You hung in there, and little by little, you began to see your child's behavior improve, at home and at school, as he or she felt understood. You also mentioned that it helped improve other relationships in your life. Way to go!

2. **You worked hard at putting your needs first.** This lesson was a tough one. It did not come naturally to you, and I saw your struggles. Saying you needed to take a nap instead of taking your child to play with Johnny or Suzy was hard because you didn't want to disappoint your child. Yet, you realized that you were in a better mood and were in a much better place when you did take your nap. Good job! You also taught your child to appreciate you and the sacrifices you make by taking care of

yourself. Several times, you told me you liked being appreciated and not taken for granted. I agree; it is a wonderful feeling.

3. **You learned about the importance of routines and how to set them up.** You began to see how the dialogues you had at home transferred to your child's schoolwork, and you asked how these would be sustained. That's when we began to talk about the importance of routines and how to set them up; you wanted these routines to turn into lifetime habits.

4. **You discovered how the skills you taught your child transfer to his/her good academic work.** When you began modeling the skills of listening and you helped your child realize that other people also matter, you truly began to work as a team with your child's teacher. You now know how the ideas and dialogues you share with your child carry over into class discussions and shape his/her own thoughts, ideas, and writing.

5. **You learned how thinking develops and how you can enrich your child's thinking by using the tools you already have.** By approaching your child at your child's level, you learned when he or she needs help understanding and how his or her mind develops. The results have been a better behaved child and better grades.

6. **Finally, you learned how to work with your child's teacher as a team.** What a wonderful lesson for both of us.

Thank you for your trust and support. Because of it, this school year was wonderful. Thank you.

Please, know that I am always here for you and your child. Contact me and let me know what doubts you have and what you would like for me to clarify. Please let me know what worked and how you made it work for you. You know my email. But just in case, here it is again:

Dana@DanaArias.com

I am hopeful that this journey, of ours, will provide us with many opportunities to talk and continue to grow. Contact me and I will give you a complimentary consultation from the point of view of a teacher, mother, and author.

I wish you and your child all the best. Thank you for being such a wonderful student.

Lovingly,
Your child's teacher
Dana M. Arias

ABOUT THE AUTHOR

Dana Arias is an author, professional speaker, parenting coach, teacher, and school librarian. Her different roles have allowed her the opportunity to speak with many parents in Texas and Illinois. These parents have come from diverse backgrounds; some have not completed high school while others hold Master's degrees. Some live below the poverty level while others enjoy a much higher standard of living. Listening closely to them has been Ms. Arias' biggest asset in helping their children.

A struggling student herself for many years, Ms. Arias has unique insight into parents' worries and concerns. Communicating and working with parents has been key to her students' development. Parents need to be seen and heard. More importantly, their needs and fears must be acknowledged. Most parents want to be central figures in their children's education. Understanding these needs, Ms. Arias has worked successfully to help bridge the distance between parents and school.

Ms. Arias has had the opportunity to partner with bilingual and general education parents in many programs established through funding by No Child Left Behind (NCLB). She has created and hosted several parent math programs, and she developed a program to teach parents how to help their children with homework, reading, and writing. She has also coordinated the NCLB program for her school and worked with parents on the Local School Council.

Raised in Mexico by an American mother and a Mexican father, Ms. Arias' bicultural and bilingual abilities are a big part of her success. Understanding both Hispanic and American cultures has been a gift for her. Being accepted and comfortable with parents from both cultures is an even greater gift. She uses the knowledge of both cultures to help parents integrate and incorporate themselves into the melting pot of her multicultural school.

Parents and students where Ms. Arias currently teaches in the Rogers Park neighborhood of Chicago represent sixty different countries and speak forty different languages at home. Helping such diverse people and cultures unite is not an easy task. Her principal has allowed her to create her own curriculum in order to help students, parents, and teachers to come together as one. The result of this work is a series of simple and easy activities parents can facilitate to connect to their children and their children's school.

Ms. Arias strives to give parents a new way to think about the relationship between home and school. Sometimes the best results come from what has always been around us, yet we are too busy to see it. Her personal and professional lives have allowed her to create from her own experiences this unique series of letters that have inspired many parents at her school. They describe her as a leader and innovator driven by the desire to facilitate meaningful interactions between students, parents, and teachers to help each child realize his or her full potential.

Ms. Arias has followed her own advice with her two teenage children and husband—even when it wasn't easy! As she shares in her letters, transformation only comes when one strives to touch that silver lining by doing the work to get there.

You can visit Dana Arias at her website:

www.DanaArias.com

COACHING

Throughout the world, a shift is happening in education. The skills our twenty-first century learners are required to master are not linear. Students need to think creatively if they are to be successful. Critical thinking and analytical skills are necessary for any type of success in our students' future endeavors. Our evolving world requires thinkers and problem solvers. Parents are aware of this need, and concern for their children's future makes them seek help, as evidenced by the number of parenting and teacher books that are published and sold every year.

Worldwide, parents are looking for the magic bullet that will transform their children into successful students. Dana Arias provides this help. Her advice is timeless, providing simple and easy to follow guidelines for parents of all ages and nationalities. No matter what country or state they live in, parents can identify with the need to discuss and share ideas that enrich their children. The challenge is knowing how to do so. Dana Arias teaches parents how to engage their children in a meaningful way that will help their grades improve. More importantly, what Dana teaches parents will allow them to prepare their children to enter a growing, specialized workforce as capable thinkers and problem solvers.

Dana's expertise is experiential—it comes from love for time spent with children. Yet, it is based on strong pedagogical foundations that she has gained through observing and studying. Her everyday interactions with parents in a simple and friendly manner have allowed her to support and guide them for the last twelve years. As a coach, her approach is easy for parents to follow—her guidelines support and nurture parents while providing small bite size pieces of information that all parents can work on in the pursuit to help their children.

For a 30 minute consultation, please contact Dana Arias at: **Dana@DanaArias.com**

BOOK DANA ARIAS TO SPEAK AT YOUR NEXT EVENT

When it comes to choosing a professional speaker at your next event, think of Dana Arias. As a straight shooter who speaks from the heart, you will find she motivates audiences into action. She does so, through wonderful real stories from her classroom experiences and her own life as a teacher and parent. She has successfully shared these experiences with hundreds of parents throughout her years of teaching.

After years of dialogue with parents, of listening to and hearing their questions, Dana Arias zeroed in on common issues that lay beneath the questions parents were asking. She came to understand and began answering these questions through an ongoing, loving, and caring series of letters written and shared at many parent-teacher conferences, at No Child Left Behind meetings, at Mother's Day recitals, and other presentations at her school. Parents responded by saying "Give us more; we need it." And she responded by creating workshops and many presentations for the parents of her school.

Now it is time to share her insight with a wider audience. Parents everywhere want what is best for their children. Teachers want what is best for their students. Both parents and teachers are screaming, "We need help!" Dana Arias provides parents and teachers with the tools to work together in creating strong students and strengthening their family's interactions.

To contact Dana Arias and book a presentation, visit her website at: **www.DanaArias.com** Or email her at: **Dana@DanaArias.com**